First published by The Word Bank in 2014.

Registered Office:
8 Jackson's Entry, Edinburgh EH8 8PJ

Design:
Emlyn Firth and Alice Rooney at a visual agency, with Edwin Pickstone at The Press.
avisualagency.com

Printing:
MLG Glasgow and DCI Print Management

A catalogue record of this book is available from the British Library.

ISBN : 978-0-9930544-0-2 | £15

9 780993 054402 >

THE
EVERGREEN

A NEW
SEASON
IN THE
NORTH

CONTENTS

CONTENTS

STARTING FROM LOCAL EXPERIENCE SEEING OUR WORLD & TAKING PART IN IT

PATRICK GEDDES 1923

For a new Evergreen to be The Word Bank's first publication could not be more appropriate. When Patrick Geddes & Colleagues published their Evergreen from Riddles Court in the Lawnmarket in 1895 and 1896, the arts of the Celtic Revival were their main sources of inspiration. They were academics and artists living in the newly created Ramsay Garden, keenly aware of the need for cultural renewal. They wished to reconnect people to literature, arts and science as part of the drive for social improvement in the Old Town.

What now inspires the Edinburgh Old Town Development Trust, the publishers of this volume, is primarily local experience: the upsurge in cooperative action evident in the growing number of Development Trusts across Scotland. Alongside growing political centralisation, there has been a flourishing of community activism—people from all walks of life working together: restoring land or buildings to productive use; providing services on behalf of local authorities; embarking on social business ventures. As Scotland debates what kind of country it wants to be, The Evergreen prompts a shifting of the question to our neighbourhoods: what kind of places do we want to live in? And what are we prepared to do about it?

Over the next two years the significance of The Evergreen heritage will be explored in four anthologies of new writing and visual art. It will urge us to look at our environment and how we relate to it. The debate about national identity must also be a question of local culture. How will citizens shape the distinctive life of their neighbourhood? In an increasingly homogenised society people are reduced to consumers of literature and art through media and the growing number of cultural spectacles. The 'arts' – our writing, singing, and painting – need to become part of our lives, to inform the way we see ourselves, our places and our future.

The Evergreen: A New Season in the North is a collaboration with the University of Aberdeen and other Scottish universities. Patrick Geddes saw education as key to social improvement, and the events programme attending each volume of The Evergreen will reflect his approach, combining the arts and sciences in a critical perspective on the way we live. As a first step we need to appreciate the differing perspectives and heritage of our neighbours. The sharing of knowledge, skills and debate will be the order of the day – common ground, shared ideals and collaborative action, the outcome.

Sean Bradley, Editor
September 2014

Editorial Board:
Sean Bradley, Elizabeth Elliott, Andrew Guest, Edward Hollis, Todd McEwen

The Word Bank is a community publishing collective run by Edinburgh Old Town Development Trust.

Edinburgh Old Town Development Trust is a Scottish charity (SC042964) committed to the revitalisation of the Old Town through stimulating growth in community participation, the arts and enterprise. It aims to support a vibrant, sustainable community in the Old Town by developing enterprising projects to meet local needs; establishing a network of gardens and green spaces; promoting education and training; and preserving the area's built and cultural heritage.

Acknowledgements:
Supported by Creative Scotland.
The work was partially funded through the Leverhulme Early Career Fellowship awarded to Elizabeth Elliott.

ALBA | CHRUTHACHAIL   The Leverhulme Trust

OLD TOWN

NEW STORY

KATE DOWNIE

9

The charcoal drawings and the subsequent etching were created in the manner of a walking/drawing conversation with the High Street of Edinburgh ten years ago. This series of street drawings were copied onto transparent acrylic then overlaid and pasted together to form multiple vanishing points and rolling perspectives. I often use direct drawing to explore geographical crossroads and borders in my work, intuiting the nature of passage and migration. Therefore the intricate nature and histories of the Old Town were perfect for this project. I am fascinated by the accumulated mark, representing countless variations of a certain archetype, including human activity in this city, its spaces traversed by locals and visitor alike. My work attempts to transform ordinary places into poetic acts of memory and in the final etching I overlaid a textured green surface, perhaps an imaginary lawn (?) appearing, like magic, over this city of stone.

Kate Downie

PROFESSOR GEDDES'S CAT

ROBERT MORRIS

17

I have been watching you for more than a hundred years now. Most of you never look up and notice me but this is a great spot looking down over the railway and the gardens. When exactly I got to be up here and who put me here I am not sure but I like watching. It is what cats do best. If you watch Princes Street for long enough you will see the whole world go by, houses rise and fall, shops come and go, marches go up and down, destruction, construction and argument. I was sorry when the steam trains went away. Arrival and departure was always a moment of excitement. But now the trams are back. The Professor would have liked that. He had a quiet admiration for the old trams. He also liked the colours of advertisements and shops. They were not quite the art of the art schools and he knew he was not supposed to like them. He was after all an active member of the Cockburn Society which was busy trying to protect the taste and appearance of the city. I have seen what he wrote about those trams. Your business, he would say, 'is not to think but to see'.

> Look at the tramway cars outside. Anyone can see more or less their ugliness, but a far more searching test of artistic progress is the measure in which we can see positive beauty. Nothing in the range of human experience promises less than those big red and yellow boxes with their advertisements. Yet set them running up and down rails, and watch how the strong foreground colour and mass of the nearest one instantly brings out the perspective of the street through its misty distance. Before it has gone two or three hundred yards you see its colour is surely somewhat changed. ... They are playing for us the game of colour these ugly cars; and with the artist we may daily find them beguile for us the dismalness of our formal street. In the same way the hoarding with its bills needs only distance to refine it; indeed as Ruskin tells us somewhere, these are now well-nigh our only source of street effect; no doubt fitly so, since the exchange of the public decorator for bill sticker, dignified, of course, as advertising contractor, is only the most obvious artistic feature of our "progress in the arts".

I often wonder how he would have got along with recent graffiti. The perpetual conflict between the authorities and the spray can hoodies would have appealed to the anarchist in him, but in the end the quality of Edinburgh graffiti is dreadful and he would have asked for help from friends in France and Germany and North America. Can the streets of Edinburgh compete or do we need to learn to look?

He did like watching people.

> Test now your colour sense upon the passing figures; say which are the more picturesque, the more intrinsically beautiful. Those gentlemen with frockcoats and tall shiny hats? Those fine ladies with new dresses so tightly stretched and strangely humped over a rudely idealized figure built outside their own? Or that poor woman, with baby wrapped in her faded shawl, and the ragged urchin turning somersaults behind the group of little girls sitting on the kerbstone?

We all prefer prosperity to poverty, he admitted, but the effect of this on shop windows was not good. The result was an 'artistic rendering in the doll-like fashion plates in the tailor and dressmakers.'

He did like his colour. I have seen some scraps of a letter he was writing to the newspapers. He did not find writing easy but the general message was clear. He had just moved into a place called James Court off the Lawnmarket. This was before he build this great palace where I am now. It was, if you will forgive an old word, a rather dreich place. The first thing he did was to slap paint around. He asked Mr Macfarlane of the Old Edinburgh Exhibition, held in the Meadows a couple of years before, what were the best colours to use.

> While securing variety of colour not only harmony but brightness has been arrived at, especially as the colour must necessarily become duller by smoke and exposure to the weather.

The object however has been by no means merely an artistic or sentimental one, although the work is still far from complete, the gain of light in all the houses in the Court is already very considerable. ... It is a familiar saying that a gas lamp is as good as a policeman but since whitewash practically doubles the value of gas lamps the gain to the public peace and safety is a real and practical one.

Hence the peculiar nonsense of saying as so many of ignorant and supercilious people especially among the worse educated members of the middle class are found doing that poor and uneducated people and children do not appreciate good surroundings.

So more colour meant better health and less crime. There was a theory behind this. It was often forgotten that he was a field biologist by training. Those people he watched on the street had brains as well as stomachs. At times he almost spoke as if the brain was more important than the stomach.

... man if he is to remain healthy and remain civilized, must not only aim at the highest standard of cerebral as well as non cerebral excellence ... but must take especial heed of his environment ... the belly and members are dominated by a brain developed and maintained through the constant and varied stimulus of the senses ... *(John Ruskin, Economist)*

The working classes, like any other, will be in well being in proportion as they become healthy organisms, leading fuller lives in richer surroundings both of art and nature, adjusted to satisfying all their needs alike. *(The Claims of Labour)*

Do not ignore the supreme needs of the brain.

There was a time when he thought that being an art critic and following Mr Ruskin was the way to reach people with his ideas but he always found art galleries frustrating and became a great man for wall murals of all kinds.

Instead of this endless labour on little panels, scattered hither and thither to flap idly upon rich men's walls, grant any of these painters one continued task for his fellow citizens, old or young – make him work for hall or school, for street or square, and see the result. ... give our friend Mr Pettie* a city hall, and see what a waking up there would be!

The Professor had a great reputation for rushing about which was somewhat unfair. He spent a lot of time looking and watching the street and the buildings of places he wrote and thought about. I remember when he came back from India with a report on the city of Indore. He had spent a lot of his time just walking and looking and learning. There was the wide street, the carts in the market place and the old palace square for parades and processions. This watching and looking taught him 'the clear cut stratification of castes' which he asked planners to respect even if they did not accept.

> In every house, but in every lane and turning, there is a record worth deciphering ... the actual human complex ... interwoven with the local history of architecture.

He always seemed to have Scottish and English cities in mind when he wrote. He thought Indore was like St Andrews, then it was Manchester or Edinburgh. Details he took from his home patch; 'set up a pigeon cote, so as to have any remaining crumbs eaten up forthwith' was his cure for rats and plague. Look just to the west of where I am and you will see he added pigeon cotes to Ramsay Garden. Not sure if there are any pigeons there now.

He searched for everyday detail by watching 'the changing and cinema like aspect of the street.' I often wonder what he would have done with moving pictures if he had started his work on cities a decade later. He had a great love of the new technologies. I remember the debate when they hired one of the new phonographs for the first time and Mrs Geddes was always insistent on

---

*John Pettie was an Edinburgh born artist. His painting *Cromwell's Saints* is in the National Gallery of Scotland collection, whilst *The Disbanded* inspired by accounts of the Jacobite defeat is in Dundee McManus Galleries.

having electricity in the new houses in Ramsay Garden. He was one of those who used photography as a way of exploring the city and he had always seen exhibitions as a way of bringing what he had found to as many people as possible. The moving film and the picture house should have been next but the years after 1916 were a terrible time. His favourite son and his dear wife died within a short time of each other and the Great War in France was not a good time for someone who believed in the positive evolution of human kind. He was never the same again after that.

Well, after more than a hundred years perched up here watching the street change, I do not get out as much as I used to do. I used to like visiting number fourteen where the Professor lived especially when he held his summer meetings but the place is closed up now and the door always locked so I don't go there any more. There are times when a cat can slip away unseen and watch the changing cinema of the street.

Professor Geddes's cat looks down on Princes Street from Ramsay Garden – no-one knows how it got there or when it goes walk about. Image by John Reiach

The quotations come from *John Ruskin Economist*, 1884; *The Claims of Labour*, 1886; *Everyman his own art critic at the Manchester Exhibition*, 1887; *Everyman his own art critic Glasgow Exhibition*, 1888. The Indore report was published in 1916. My thanks as ever to Mr Simon Bolam, secretary of the Ramsay Garden Residents Association, who introduced me to Professor Geddes's cat.

POEMS

BENJAMIN MORRIS

NANCY SOMERVILLE

ANDREW MᶜDOUGALL

25

OROGRAPHY
Arthur's Seat, for Dacia

Step to step, flight to flight,
the years I'd hoped to write
pass underneath our weary feet.
The summit rises to greet

us with the dawn; so long
since you've climbed a mountain
that you've forgotten how — lagging
a dozen paces behind, flagging

the gap that lays between us
with an old, familiar silence.
The sound is louder than the din
of the world below, or the winds

crowding out our breath.
This is — we were — not a test,
I want to say, but every time
the words come into reach, the climb

takes a sudden, inward turn,
the stones seeking to unlearn
us, to keep us from the top.
You take my hand for the final step:

to raindrops echoing in pools,
the clouds around us unspooling
their liquid thread, saying what
this jagged path of words could not.

Benjamin Morris

CARTOGRAPHY

And there we were,
out of breath, of blood in our legs,
but alive at the top of the city
whose streets splayed out
like the veins on the backs
of our hands. Down below
we had not known how silent
they truly were, how our words
rose clean as mist from the earth,
carried off by the wind
by the time we climbed up
to meet them.
       Were we to stand there
and draw a map of this town,
we could sketch the squares
we drifted through like leaves,
the park bench, lost in a thicket
of tongues, where we found the stories
to guide us home. Let them not
slip away like the names
of the lanes that tried to lose us,
even this road at the end of the day,
where I walk slowly down a hall,
hoping to hear a door breathe open
behind me, see the night
flowing through your hair.

Benjamin Morris

NOCTURNE: LOS ANGELES
Ben Aronson, 1998

As though this city ever woke.
   Here light only skirts the canvas,
dashing off the palette in haste
   from the darkness billowing like a flame,
whose tufts and sprays shimmer
   and breathe before our eyes —

even color is an afterthought,
   daubs of cobalt and rose
dotting the lyric black,
   smears left behind as a reminder
of what the day vainly authored:
   flecks of speckled buildings

on the horizon, dark architectures
   rising despite the lights inside them,
long arcs of distant cars
   curving off the edge of the frame
past the charcoal ghosts of palms
   casting their shadows on the shade

where overhead, two faint streaks
   prepare for their descent
into a city that barely stirs,
   only dreams anew through the night,
its indigo face a lake
   in which all our dreams will drown.

Benjamin Morris

JOHNSTON TERRACE
3rd October 2010

We are grounded,
too intent on gutter-gazing
to soar. We lean over the wall
not seeing what's before us,
peering down through the canopy
of autumn leaves,
into the locked garden
twenty feet below.

We slowly realise
we're in them,
the treetops we think
block our view,
level with birds and berries,
fruits of the roots
which grip soil and rock,
holding onto the history
of this place.

Nancy Somerville

THE SHADOW OF
THE SIDE ACROSS
i.m. William Fraser (1880-1917)

He woke uneasy and disturbed
As though some passing ghost
Had riven him from vital troubles
And dropped him back
Into that August night.
The hottest of the year.

Dawn blazed a bar across the half-pulled blind
Above the shadow of the side across.
Windows wide against the heat.
Familiar noises of the old South Side
Pressed into his waking mind,
And hinted at the town beyond.

The rising rattle of the first few trams;
A distant bark;
Sad horses making early rounds;
And the faraway voices of distracted men
Embarking on grim business.
And with those sounds the smells of home,
Of simple food and coal tar, safety, comfort.
His wife lay sleeping still beside him
The sleek dark bell-rope of her hair.
Her cinnamon and roses.
He turned towards her body's lovely lines,
Her easy curving hip, the cool weight of her breasts.
He took a deeper breath and saw,
On her pale neck, small hairs arise.

The fleeting shadow of a bird in flight
Crossed the white bar of the blind and dropped
To the falling shadow of the side across.

He rose to clear his head and cool himself
Put bare feet to cold boards
And stood watch for his sleeping bairns.
The solemn baby in her cot,
Across the box-bed spread the others,
Thrown, abandoned, to the night,
Tangled pale and slender limbs,
Dampened curls. Over each
In turn he drew his breath
To hold the moment back.

He stopped before the yellow blind
As the falling shadow of the side across
Gave way at last to rising sun
And white light flooded, filled the place.

Andrew McDougall

(N)EVERGREEN?

AULD

REEKIE

ABSOLVED

RICHARD RODGER

In 1771, David Hume and sixteen of his New Town neighbours sought to halt building development on the 'pleasure gardens' to the south side of Princes Street. Their amenity was compromised, they claimed, and their view of the Castle threatened. It was a dispute with the developer – the Town Council – that resulted in a compromise. The plots already built up to the line of the Waverley Steps, as we now know it, would be retained; westwards no further building was permitted.

The compromise was the result of a Court of Session decision, reversed by the House of Lords in 1772, and signalled the beginning of almost half a century of legal disputes[1]. At issue was the potential damage to property owners' substantial housing investment caused by uncontrolled development on adjoining plots. What was the point, as owners noted, of spending £3500 or more on a town house if there was no guarantee that nuisances such as the production of noxious fumes were permissible next door? The concept of 'nichterbourheid', which enshrined the right to challenge practices that adversely affected the light, smell, and access caused by adjoining property owners, was weakly defended by a largely toothless Dean of Guild Court in the eighteenth century. 'Nimbyism', therefore, was alive and well in Enlightenment Edinburgh, and the specific issue raised by Hume and his friends was only resolved in 1818 when Lord Eldon ruled that to 'infer' that sight of James Craig's plan for the New Town was 'unsafe and ambiguous' as a basis upon which to decide what could be built upon a plot. Lord Eldon explained that to do so 'would be as violent a stretch in judicature as ever I met in the course of a long professional life.'

Lord Eldon's decision fundamentally recast conveyancing practice. A plan – in fact every plan – was unreliable because of its two-dimensional ambiguity; only words could explain the precise limitations placed on the use, height, form, and features of what could be built on a plot. These 'burdens' or restrictions were to be specifically created and identified in feu charters, and applied in perpetuity and on subsequent subdivisions of the plot. Annual feu duties became a commodity when sold as 'heritable securities' for up to thirty times their annual value. Lord Eldon's judgment reassured owners about their investment, boosted their confidence in property development, and created a financial

---

[1] For further details of this 50 year conflict over property rights and the James Craig plan for Edinburgh see R. Rodger, The Transformation of Edinburgh: Land, Property and Trust in the Nineteenth Century (Cambridge pbk. 2004), 62-8.

instrument based purely on ownership of a plot. Scottish urban land values increased to levels only exceeded in central London, a condition recognised as such when rent controls were introduced in the twentieth century.

The Scottish tenement form was reinforced as a result. The nimbyism of the New Town dwellers' campaign ensured that expensive land resulted in intensive multi-storey development of plots. The smoke-blackened new walled canyons of tenements in Fountainbridge, Tollcross, Causewayside, Dalry, Easter Road, lower Canongate, and south Leith were the principal habitats of Edinburgh's industrial workforce. The soft tenement sandstones of Mid- and West Lothian, together with those of Northumbria, were saturated with the sooty deposits of gasworks, breweries, foundries, wood-working workshops, as well as the lums of sixteen-in-a-block flats, and the railway engines that hauled freight to and fro on the spaghetti of railway lines that penetrated the city. So pervasive was smoke pollution even as early as 1855 that 112 businesses were served with nuisance orders in an effort to mitigate the impact on the lungs of Edinburgh citizens. Drab districts threatened to become a feature of 'Auld Reekie' as intensive plot development resulted in a new form of feudalism in which the role of superior and vassal were reasserted by Lord Eldon's judgment. Would Edinburgh never be green?

If, as contemporary photographs show, the overwhelming impression of the Old Town and Victorian industrial suburbs was one of smoked-stained façades, the seven green hills of Modern Athens provided a healthy escape for those who had leisure time to enjoy them. Also for the wealthy, individual rear gardens and key access to shared green space in the city centre provided places for perambulation and quiet contemplation. A similar degree of peace was possible in Edinburgh churchyards from the 1860s when all except St. Cuthbert's were closed for burials, displaced as they were by six shareholder owned cemetery companies covering almost 60 acres established on the periphery of the city in the 1840s[2]. Swathes of institutionally owned space to the west also provided a green girdle around the city – from Donaldson's Hospital via John Watson's and the Dean Orphanage to the Inverleith lands of Rocheid (Botanical Gardens and Inverleith Park) and the playing fields of

---

[2] P. Laxton and R. Rodger, Insanitary City: Henry Littlejohn and the Condition of Edinburgh (2013), 146-55.

Edinburgh Academy, Fettes and Heriot's. Green space was also increasingly available through the development of 14 (mostly) private golf courses between 1890 and 1914 (see table), and a several major public parks.

Table 1 : The Development of Golf Courses in Edinburgh

COURSE	YEAR	COURSE	YEAR
Royal Burgess	1735	Murrayfield	1896
Bruntsfield	1761	Turnhouse	1897
Portobello	1853	Kingsknowe	1908
Craigentinny	1891	Carricknowe	1905
Mortonhall	1892	Merchants	1907
Braids	1893	Ravelston	1912
Lothianburn	1893	Prestonfield	1920
Baberton	1893	Liberton	1920
Duddingston	1895	Swanston	1927
Craigmillar Park	1895	Silverknowes	1957
Torphin	1895		

Public parks were a relatively late development in Edinburgh compared to many English industrial cities. Of course customary use of public spaces such as Leith Links (a public park from 1888) and the Meadows were noted as a 'lung' for 'the working classes' and for their organised cricket matches, so much so that there were protests when in 1886 the Meadows were appropriated for the Edinburgh International Industrial Exhibition and the 2.8 million visitors who trampled over the hallowed turf. However, as the city population doubled from 68,000 in 1801 to 168,000 in 1861, and with its new unitary authority status after 1856, the Town Council gradually sought to extend its boundaries into what was the contemporary equivalent of the 'green belt.' Blackford (1884); Harrison (1886); Inverleith (1889); Roseburn (1889); and Saughton (1900) parks were amongst the most extensive creations. But there were determined efforts to create new smaller scale parks and to take existing ones in the inner city into public management too – Gayfield Square (1886), Starbank (1889), Iona/Dalmeny Street (1902). In these and other public parks, *The Scotsman* (5th May 1896, p.6), noted that the 'Town Council has done much to encourage this quiet, enjoyable pastime' (bowling), and commented: 'nowhere in Scotland has the game made more rapid progress during the last few years.' A charge to use bowling greens of 1d per hour per person was levied, and in the wet summer of 1895 exactly 57,646 pennies (£240 3s.10d or £24,210 adjusted to 2013 prices) were collected. There were thirty Bowling Clubs in Edinburgh with a combined membership of over 1800 in 1896, and four in Leith; no individual was allowed to play for more than an hour and 'there were many casual players not connected with any club.' The newspaper commented positively about the initiative of the Corporation 'for putting this healthy means of outdoor recreation within the reach of so many', though they were also admonished for the poor quality of the turf.

Overall, the development of a high-density nineteenth-century city with its associated adverse environmental implications for health and life expectancy became a sensitive issue in the last decades of the nineteenth century. Many agencies – individual, institutional, public, and charitable – sought to address the consequences of congested living and even private builders, by providing drying greens encased behind the walls of the newly built tenements in industrial districts, added proportionately to the amount of open space available. Just as there was greenery behind the exclusive New Town flats in Great King Street and Eton Terrace, so in rectangular shared spaces behind the continuous tenemented streets of Dalry – Cathcart, Springwell and Downfield Places, and many others like them – 'greens' were part of the standard design.

So Patrick Geddes' initiatives to develop urban gardens in the city centre were consistent with, and indeed were anticipated by a variety of other greening actions. As for timing and impact, the Open Spaces Committee of the

Outlook Tower Association noted, 'Since commencing work in the Autumn of 1908 nine gardens have been laid out, two being in the Canongate, and others in the Castlehill and Grassmarket neighbourhoods.'[3] Their extent was limited, and usage unknown. Where Geddes' contribution was more explicit, however, was in recognising and publicising the relationships between biodiversity, accessibility, and creativity in a modern city.

---

[3] I am grateful to Lou Rosenburg for information on this point.

POSTCARDS FROM A HILL TOWN

JOHN REIACH

POEMS

JOHN MᶜGLADE

~~~

IAN MᶜDONOUGH

~~~

PETER KRAVITZ

~~~

45

BLADE

Blade of grass
Up, up in high Asia
feels the gravitational pull of world,
            regional and local superpowers

in perfect balance

Blade of grass
the only living thing
standing its full height

John McGlade

METEOR SHOWER

At first we'd hoped the haze
might die beyond the city.
We drew in at a lay-by,
killed the headlamps,
gazed up at impenetrable mist.

A squad car pulled along,
driven by a different curiosity:
"Going far Sir? Everything OK?
Meteor Showers? Had a drink?"

Aiming back for Edinburgh's lights
silence absorbed us, imagining
these tracer patterns high above the earth,
illuminating everything, revealing nothing.

Ian Mcdonough

DEBORAH WARNER'S 'EUGENE ONEGIN', 2011

He arrives   she glances   they stroll   they dine   she tells   he leaves
he returns   she asks   he refuses   they stroll   they do not touch   they talk   they talk
he leaves
he asks   they dance   he sees   he rages   he accepts   she moves   he moves
they kiss

she cannot write   she cannot wait
she cannot   she
he wakes   he duels   he kills   he leaves
he travels   he forgets   he drifts   he wishes   he wanders   he roams

she aches   she stares into the fire

she marries

she continues

she lingers

they are gathering
they are drinking
they are dancing
he appears   he yawns   he looks   he remembers   he regrets
he asks   he follows   he glances   she smiles   she resists
she leaves   he writes   he waits   she reads
she waits   she sinks

he returns
he confesses
she insists
he denies
she tells   he begs   he assures
he implores   she refuses   she recalls   he repeats   she endures
he pleads   she falters
he repeats   they touch   he kisses   she kisses   she turns   she walks
he cries.

Peter Kravitz

WOMAN PAINTING

While they were running out for break, she held her eyes
onto the well of ink,
the wood, the metal bracket
the four-times-folded sweetie paper.

To questions her laugh trimmed to a smile
opening to spaces, places
mixing up
the must be thises for it could be thats.

Finding plenties without looking she coasts inside
her ears her nose
her thumbs her toes
no stickyout bit was left uncovered.

Some grew hard bits, these took them under
she sprouted sponge and brush, these took her over.

This grey is not a blue.

She walks the fogs to get the colours home
the pigments then assembled rub against each other.

Each swifty landing on this canvas turns
what was to what's meant to be.

By letting sounds come through
she can condense a lot
she rips her flow.

There's no man's mouth, no red around the nose
no right no left no him at all no her.

She keeps on coming back to marks.

Peter Kravitz

ROGER HILTON'S 'RED SEA', 1958

looking into me is easy I am made for that

under glass you sit a red boat on a red sea
smaller than you seem bigger than you are
watching others warm your surface, I want you home

should I worry when someone comes across to part us
or that I get you more when I'm away
or that I might make things end before they begin
or that I can't see there's weather outside

I do not move, I wait on strangers to sherpa me
you can have me, you can follow without stalking, look without flirting

I'm texting HEY I'M FALLING FOR THIS BOAT
my eyes may rest on you and my praise pressure you, but keeping them
corrodes

give me something so I know I dent you,
stick me in your memory, take   me   home

I tap tap my screen, grab and pull and blow you up,
then lose you to the pixels

fussturr disprey grabyark, I've let them out
I don't have many, help me back to meaning without words

I leave my eyes on you too long, now I join your debtors
how can you keep on giving

with so many galleries, your look will be tempted

when I'm back home and ping a meal
the dimmers light your pigment, infareds coast in to take you over

you may come to see me differently
I might tell the paper: PIER CENTRE BOAT PIC IN SNUB SHOCK

you're asking me
to leave the things I thought I knew.

Peter Kravitz

ARTIST OF THE NATURAL WORLD

DOMINIC COOPER

Light lies forever exploding in the eye, searing itself into mind and memory. Its burst may be violent and lancing and as brittle as a soundless glass-shatter. At other times it may lie quiet, a mere glintering upon the darkness of a mountain lochan or a sheltered arm of the sea. Then again, still further removed from all obvious images of brightness, you may come upon it hanging swollen and dim in the dusk of a day, seeming no more than some inner refulgence of the air, like a reverberation of a thing lost and only half-recalled. Even in the middle of a dull winter's day, with the sky but a flat, grey mash, light has always offered us reassurance of hope, just as a single candle flame burning steady in the night may at times be all that represents our trust in a future.

This guardian friendship of light must stand first: without it, there can be no hope. But with light comes colour. And if light may be seen as the emblem of our grit strength of survival, so the whole tradition of colour symbolises our experience of emotion, of the joy and pain in our lives: vivid, primal colours echoing the sensations of elation and power, of everything that drives us forwards. With all the darker hues there come up images of threat and weight and foreboding; whereas in the paler tones we feel ourselves being drawn into areas of peace and calm. In all colours, be they dense and heavy or the most washed-out and muted of tints, there will be some suggestion, some indelible reflection of old memory.

When one considers colour and how, until quite recently, it was always made from vegetable and mineral dyes, it reminds us just how, from the very beginning, our whole vision of colour has been informed by the natural world around us. What colour might there be, one wonders, that does not already grow on some hillside, or in some wood, or in a distant corner of the sky? However we may come to the creation of a colour, it would seem that we can never invent it: nature has somehow always been there before us. And perhaps in this there lies a connecting truth, an understanding that nature has preceded us not simply in this but in everything. And a thought that we would forget this at our peril. For all our technical wizardry and achievement, we cannot escape the fact that our ancestry, our whole make-up and origins, will always demand that we acknowledge our roots in the natural world.

It is, among other things, some sort of awareness of this need that brings people—and not least artists— to live in the country. Out there, on the hills or perhaps overlooking the sea under huge skies, we find clues as to our true being. Perspectives of the open hill give us guidance as to just where we are in relation to the world, perhaps even to eternity. They remind us that while each of us may be unique, we are at the same time all but irrelevant, vital on the smallest of scales and yet immeasurably disposable in the greater span. The blowing up and the passing of storms, the polished-out doming of a clear winter sky, the midsummer afterlight, the calm sweetness of drizzle, a sudden epiphany of light breaking through dark cloud, the blossomburst of spring — even perhaps the sight of some miniscule plant, some tiny fists of fire, say, couched in a dank corner of a wood, known otherwise only by mouse and vole — these are the waymarkings that so often give proportion to our day-to-day living.

One of the cornerstones of spending time close to nature is a realisation that it all exists of itself and owes nothing to us and our machinations, that it will continue to proceed as ever, willy-nilly through the years, irrespective of whether or not we ourselves, ingenious and ignorant creatures that we are, manage to survive. In the quietness of this knowledge it is easier to appreciate what we stand to lose and harder to understand the sheer scale of man's wayward behaviour in relation to the natural world.

Landscape and colour, light and the shape of our passing lives — all artists will in some way sense the way the patterns interlock. But the true one, the complete artist — such a rare thing — will also be a visionary, somebody who can see beyond the simple format of things, who is able to draw in and encompass a greater sense of what lies just beyond and beneath that which is there and visible before us. In the world of artistic creation, is this element what we lamely refer to as 'the meaning' of a work? And more generally, much in the way that the eye seems to look for the distant vanishing point in a picture, is this the half-sensed truth that draws us on in our lives? Matter vanishing into spirit, becoming the knowledge forever just out of sight, just beyond our grasp, as in the dream?

Standing within a landscape is a ritual involvement with the physical world, an involvement which is vital in that it mirrors and at the same time defines our spiritual position in relation to the earth. The artist of the natural world instinctively knows this and goes on applying himself to the task of its inter-pretation, shaping and re-shaping this crucial conundrum in support of us other benighted souls who may have lost the power of inner vision, the ability to see beyond and within, where there has always lain truth and succour. Whether artist, magus or otherwise, the visionary's rôle is to be the descendant of the shaman who in earlier times would cross backwards and forwards between the here and the beyond by means of the dangerous bridge, the tree, the vine or the cord. He or she a chosen one, guardian of the secret without which all our spirits would eventually wither and perish.

There is a myth that the chief need of all artists is to communicate, to convey their truths to the rest of the world. At least that is what the rest of the world has apparently always liked to think — and artists haven't usually bothered to say otherwise. But what in fact the artist is looking for first and foremost is quite another sort of dialogue, one that is essentially between himself and his other self. It is this inner dialogue, often involving the confrontational meeting of opposites, that creates tension, a good tension, which makes the artist's work strong and so of interest to the public.

Much in the way that the child seems to slip so naturally between its waking and its fantasy worlds, so must the artist live forever straddling two worlds of consciousness — the outer, visible self keeping constantly in touch with the inner and dreaming spirit. That is the only format available for an artist's proper functioning: indeed since it's the only way he knows of getting by, it comes close to being his reason for living. Bereft of it, his psychic whole soon starts to fragment.

Some artists, those whose whole living and breathing is inextricably close-coupled with their spirit life, find the need for this dialogue so acute that town living, with its opportunities for fame and financial reward, must be put aside, simply because of the overwhelming nature of urban clutter and stramash. These people, these makers of symbols, these dreamers of the mysteries, must find for themselves a way of living and working in the quiet of the countryside. For it is only here, sometimes deep in the tumultuous serenity of wilderness, that the silent speech can truly be heard.

We hold the rounded pebble and, closing our eyes, slowly begin to feel its sheen take on the warmth of our hand. We find ourselves wanting to close our fist around it ever more fiercely, almost as if to try and make it part of ourselves. Or perhaps we will be happy to balance it lightly between thumb and forefinger, and hold it up to look at against the sky where we can see it making up the missing part of a circle of forces. Even when later consigned to a pocket, we'll probably keep going back to it, stroking it blindly with a dull awareness of what such a small smooth thing might represent, as a talisman in itself but also as a symbol of the earth that is beneath us, the earth which we think of as ours but to which we in fact belong.

We hold the pebble. Or, lying on the grass high under the sun, on a hillside hanging far above the hush of the sea, we may suddenly feel impelled to roll over and bury our faces in the soil. For the sheer joy of it, as it were, but also for the dizzying thought of our origins among the centuries of rock and sleeping power lying unfathomed beneath.

These images, of our bond with the enduring earth, are merely the symbols of the secret dialogue. For spirit and earth, dreaming and rock, are not in the end separate things. If such an idea does not quite fit in with or is not fully comprehensible to our oversharpened digital minds, it is no great surprise. Indeed, for all that we have succeeded in proving to finality so much of our world, our full understanding of the deeper whys and the wherefores of things has always remained woefully incomplete.

Wandering the open land, searching for clues, the shifting focus of one's eye slips effortlessly between the vast and the diminutive. How many times has one looked up from examining a rock-borne fleck of lichen, a glowing bud of moss, and seen, high above, the great eternities of sky bursting and riven by unworldly shapes of cloud and light? Somewhere, within the balance created by the tension of opposites, lies the gateway through.

MARCAS MAC AN TUAIRNEIR

OWEN O'NEILL

BOGHA CHLANN UIS

Fosgail, a m' uinneig don speuran.
Brist ioma-chrith na tìm is talmhainn
Is seall dhomh an saineas,
Eadar comasachd is miann.

'S thusa clàr shùilean is cholainn;
Gach ceathramh ar domhain.
Geàrraidh mi sgrìob thuca,
Gun ach òdan air putan.

Abair, gur mi tha pòsta
Aig gach gin àraid aca.
Ann an cruinne-cè co-shìnte,
A' sireadh chothroman eadar-dhealaichte.

Ach san roinn seo,
Suidhidh mi air an t-sòfa,
No anns an taigh-seinnse,
A' feitheamh ri freagairt,
Bho bheul an aineolais.

Agus fhad 's a strìochdas
Gach coltas don dorchadas is
Ghealladh nas danarra;
Saoil...

A bheil fleasgach ri sporadh
Na h-iarmailt,
Son boillsgeadh m' aire-sa,
Làn dòchais is follais,
Ri speuradaireachd.

Marcas Mac an Tuairneir

THE MILKY WAY

Open, my window to the stars.
Break earthquake in time and territory
And show me the diversity
Between possibility and fancy.

You grid of eyes and chests; all
Quadrants of our universe.
I'll cut a route through to them,
With mere fingertip on button.

They say I am married
To each one in their exclusivity,
In each universe laid parallel,
Pursuing different chances.

But on this plane,
I sit on the setée,
Or in a hostelry,
Suspended on response
From the mouth of ignorance.

And as each likeness succumbs
To the darkness
And a bolder promise;
I wonder...

If there's a fellow fumbling
Through the firmament,
For the glimmer of my devoir,
Full of hope and openness
In his stargazing.

Marcas Mac an Tuairneir

HEANEY AMONG THE TREES

With that gear shift, he lifted me then in the trees high
above Derryloran . I could hear and see the lorry.
No man before had put me so firmly in my place, told me
who I was and where I was from.

Forgotten days, remembered for me, whether I wanted
them or not. The distant unfamiliar hum at the very top
of the horse chestnut. One slip and I was gone. The danger
of going as far as I could.

My Father saying 'You always go too far boy' But to look at
the familiar from a dangerous place, that's what I was
striving for. That's why Heaney was always among the trees
to get a sense of what it is we are, what it is we really want,

what it is we love. To grab on for dear life, to go further
up and up and up, one foot after the other. To sit then
in the silence of ourselves with everything beneath us.
One slip and we're gone.

Owen O'Neill

MOTHER AND CHILD

Their faces in profile, and there
Is no doubt, the nose, the mouth
aligned through centuries.

She sits, her hands in her lap
nothing out of place, whilst he
cuts the meat on her plate.

She is not ashamed, and he
is not hurried in this task. Her
eyes are bright, her skin, dropping

velvet, lined and dignified. Small
rubies catch the light and sparkle
on her open neck.

She had cut his meat, washed his
every crevice, knew all the moves
he had made, was ever going to make.

His turn now and he performs it with
love and tenderness. Time on her hands,
she picks up the fork, the food moving slowly

towards her mouth, travelling through time
from her Wedding day, to his birth, to this
moment and back again.

This was what she had, what she had built
a son, to love her quietly, by this river, in this
restaurant, on a Sunday.

Owen O'Neill

EXPECTING TO GIVE

LEILA ABOULELA

65

The sun tilts toward me but there is a cold wind. I can see it through the window, bouncing the pink petals on the trees. I spend the mornings in bed to put off that first standing up which makes me nauseous. The doctor says I should try eating a cracker before I get up, but it doesn't work. I walk to the bathroom and I'm sick in the basin. White froth and then with further retches it turns smooth and dark yellow like cough medicine, only bitter. Then back into bed sweaty and hungry.

Saif's been away eight days and nine hours. He's not due back until next week. I can't phone him unless there's an emergency. They don't like personal phone calls on the rigs and he's not allowed to take his mobile phone because it's against the regulations. I'm floppy without him. He is excited and confident about the baby while I wade through the days. Tomorrow I go to my first ultrasound appointment at the hospital. Husband offshore, parents in another country, not a single friend to accompany me.

I thought pregnancy meant radiant skin and a stomach to be proud of. But I am barely showing and held back by waves of sleep; anxieties about the baby, about the birth, about the world I hear about on the news. Whenever Saif comes home we dwell on the changes in my body. Only a swell below my navel but my breasts are bigger. Sometimes they hurt, a dull pleasant ache, a gradual heaviness.

Hunger like I have never experienced. I stare at the ceiling and know that, if necessary, I can fight someone for food and I can rummage through garbage looking for titbits. It is something I did not know about myself. The baby is a parasite, the pregnancy book says, the baby will take from you all that he needs. Well, the baby seems to need eggs with ketchup, beans with ketchup, crisps with ketchup... so this is what a craving is, I realize, this passion for tomatoes, their redness and taste. Yesterday it was stale bread with ketchup, and when the bread ran out, just one spoonful after the other.

This is the most difficult challenge, getting out of bed. Not getting up to vomit and coming back but getting up to have a shower and dress. If I am going to cry it will be now, first thing in the morning with the nausea in my chest and the day stretching out ahead.

It's not fair, is it, that Saif has taken me away from my career, my friends, my family and brought me here only to leave me and go off-shore? But I am being irrational. It is his work and I should be supportive. I had walked into this marriage with eagerness, with eyes wide open. My parents were becoming stifling, my friends boring and my womb, fertile and unattended, was eager to flourish and enclose. I did not want to sink into my thirties, to reach the desperate stage and acquire that expectant stalking look.

Saif was the nicest of them all, fresh and honest in an irresistible way. Marriage was a good move, coming here the right choice. It's not a raw deal; it's actually a good package. Yes, the bad weather, the loneliness when Saif goes off-shore but when he is here it is like a holiday; one honeymoon after the other. In the two-weeks that he is onshore we stay up late, we have breakfast at lunchtime, we go to the cinema, we go out shopping. It is nice to be able to afford things, not to have to skimp and save. He is generous really, when he is freezing on the wretched rig working night shifts he keeps himself going by repeating, 'Think of the bonus, think of the baby, think of the bonus.' I have a lot to thank Allah for, instead of crying.

I bribe myself with breakfast so that I can get through the shower. I toast bread and make an omelette with feta cheese and the necessary tomatoes. I put more tomatoes than eggs, more tomatoes than cheese. It is mysterious this craving, too intense to be explained away by a need for Vitamin C. Even the pregnancy books are unsure. They say it is hormones that will only settle at fourteen weeks but that doesn't explain why I have suddenly gone off coffee and can't live without tomato juice.

The post brings more rejection letters. All the job applications I sent out when I first moved here are bouncing back. But do I have the audacity to turn up to an interview pregnant? These days I am sick or asleep, restless for a specific taste, hiding from toxic scents real and imaginary. I clean the bathroom with ordinary soap to avoid harsh detergents, in the supermarket I bypass certain rows.

I drive to the kebab shop for lunch. Driving is a triumph for me, a reminder that I am not completely helpless, completely housebound. It is a throwback to my past single life, the career woman with the little car, with somewhere to go, very busy. In another part of the world I had been a social worker. I identified children at risk and set up a programme to rehabilitate teenage drug addicts. I have to stop the car and vomit in a paper cup. Nothing comes out but white froth, my breakfast has fast disappeared. It is an empty stomach than makes me sick, though it is hard to believe. When I am full, the nausea goes away. But I am digesting too fast. I can hardly hold myself back between one meal and the next. Traffic whizzes past me. I wipe my mouth with tissues and stuff them in the paper cup. It suddenly feels too warm in the car, I open the window, indicate and drive out.

The smell of the shop pleases me. I need the large kebab sandwich, the salad soaked in chilli. I ask for ketchup too. Ketchup on the tomatoes, ketchup soaking the bread and the meat. It runs down the side of my mouth. A slim woman pushes her way through the door. It rattles so hard that most of us look up. Her deranged hair is streaked blonde, her nose bruised red; she is not steady on her feet. She stands at the door trembling. "Marouf," she hisses. 'Marouf.' The youngest of the staff, handsome enough for Bollywood, rushes to her side, tries to lead her by the arm out to the street. She holds her ground, 'You LIED to me. You did ... You told me you'd be back, you told me ... Come home ...' She's whining now and the rest of the staff are hiding their sniggers.

Marouf's face is dark with embarrassment. He tilts his head and squeezes her arm. His voice is too low for me to hear his replies. She starts to hurl abuse at him, one ek sound after the other. When he tries to push her out the door she cuffs his face. This relieves her momentarily and he is able to dislodge her into the street. The door clinks behind them. I squeeze more ketchup onto my salad. I finish my sandwich and my drink. Marouf comes back in and his work mates taunt him in a language I don't understand. The ketchup has run all over my plate and I don't have a spoon to lap it up.

No longer hungry, I feel fine. The fresh air is doing me good. I hurry past Starbucks, the merest whiff of coffee threatens a nausea attack. Strange that I used to malfunction without two black coffees a day, now how to explain this sensitivity to smells? The foetus protecting itself from the dangers of coffee is a proposition but then not every pregnant woman has the same response.

I walk into a mother and baby store and wish that it wasn't too early to buy maternity clothes. I touch the baby products. Soft yellows and blues and pink. Cuddly toys, terry cloth; cots and bubble bath. I pick up a bottle of baby oil and breathe in the scent. It fills me with wellness, with innocence; baby sweetness and joy. The baby clothes for girls are nicer than the ones for boys. This time tomorrow, after the ultrasound, will I know if my baby is a he or a she? I can't want a boy or want a girl, it is already predetermined, it is already, thrillingly, too late. I am carrying a brand new creation, a beauty to cuddle, a precious name, a fresh personality whose steps I will share. Next to me a woman, about eight months pregnant, is looking at the plastic baths. Her stomach is like a basket ball that had fallen once on her lap, her navel is inside out, protruding against her T-shirt. I feel like I am in primary school looking up in awe at one of the senior girls. I buy vitamins and a cream for stretch marks. I buy two new bras. Saif will want to check out the car seat and the stroller. He will revel in all the baby gadgets, locks and mobiles – I smile thinking we will come here together.

Outside, I find myself face to face with the woman from the kebab shop. This time she is pushing a toddler in a pushchair and staring into the shop window. The little boy's hair is so long that the fringe is almost covering his eyes. She must have left him outside the kebab shop, I realize, he must have been all alone on the pavement all the time she and Marouf were having their fight! The baby sits straight up clutching his foot with one hand and a packet of crisps in the other; some of it falls to the ground.

It is because of him that I speak to her. 'I saw you back at the kebab shop. Are you all right now?' I bend to smile at her son. He looks at me and makes a lovely ga sound, his own distinctive voice, his few teeth sitting lonely in their gums. I want to lift him up, to bathe him, to feed him, to teach him. I am yearning for my own baby and my silent invisible swell of a stomach is a solemn promise, the secret I am waiting to share. Beyond the fog of lethargy and nausea, after the heaviness and the pain, I will look down at an infant in my arms. She will be the centre of my life, she will be in focus, in colour and everything around her will be blurred, in black and white. I reach out to touch the toddler's hair. It is so pale that it is almost white. Surely he is too fair to be Marouf's. Surely. I am judging his mother now and as if she can read my mind, she withdraws, her face grim. Without a word, she yanks the pushchair so that the poor child is jerked back into his seat.

"Wait," I say but she is walking faster. I catch up with her and she is forced to stop. My words come out in a rush, "You should give him a rusk or a piece of fruit, not this snack that is not even potatoes! Get him something good. He needs proper food to grow. And cut his fringe, he can barely see through it..."

'I don't need you interfering! Mind your own bloody business.' She pushes down on the handlebars so that the pushchair jerks up and comes down on my toes. I stand rooted to the pain as she flounces off. And because I haven't spoken to anyone for days, I feel sorry for myself. I wipe my tears and hobble to the car. I used to have a gaggle of friends and invitations to parties; at work others listened when I made presentations, I even had an assistant in my last few months before I resigned. In that other past life, I never craved tomatoes and I must have passed one hard-done-by mother after the other without turning a hair.

Saif is getting out of a taxi just as I am parking my car. It is such a surprise that I almost bump the curb and forget to undo my seat belt. 'Careful', he calls out as he lifts his rig bag from the boot and pays off the taxi. He is smiling and tousled like he always is when he first comes home, still with the noise of the machines ringing in his ears, the unsteadiness of the platform, the stinging wind of the North Sea. Now he can put all this behind him and have everything he's been looking forward to. How perfect of him to be here today! I need the weight of his arms, his voice telling me off, his fingers rummaging through the things I just bought. I run into his arms. He explains that there's been a false alarm at the rig and non-essential staff for the ongoing operation were evacuated as a precaution. Lucky for me he was one of them. He is still in his rig coveralls and the smell of the oil pushes its way up my nose, black grease down my throat, fumes in my gullet. I move my face as a burp turns into a gag, into a retch.

"What's wrong?" He holds me but I twist away. I stagger to the side of the road and aim my mouth at the nearest bushes. The ground is pink with fallen cherry blossoms. "It's the smell," I splutter. "I'm sorry. It's not you. Don't be hurt."

He is though, a little. It's in his voice when he says, "We'll be together tomorrow at the hospital for the ultrasound."

This does make me feel better. The nausea ebbs and I want to doze off, just for a short nap. Tomorrow after the appointment, we can go for lunch in town. Pizza, this time. Pizza with extra tomatoes.

POEMS

DAVID HERD

73

i.
I am holding my heart in my cheeks as the Americans say.
His absence is what the birds the waxwings sing about.
I can be straight about this
My method is to cut things out.
Days later I left a voicemail.
If you can
Call me.

As trees are my witness, the result was not anticipated.
They are right to observe the lyric is relational.
I count
Such shapes
Up in the streets the underground
No unpaid debts
This evening in the universe.

ii.
I come back to it.
The lyric is the new geography.
I take this to be normal emotional
That all the co-ordinates are good.
Like that thrush
Picked up across the street
Aspects of a person's circumstance
Speaking plainly
It was a moment of intense legality.

What we're talking about of course
Is a genuine and subsisting relationship.
I count such shapes.
The truth of all such impasses

Is one has not found the form
And so I come back to it
The elementary mistake
Of translating 'we' as 'they'
Giving the impression
Always maintained
Shall comprise an area.

iii.
You're looking good today I mean alive
To which we must address ourselves
As the earth turns
Trailing across the light of the sun
Which is one of the things I love
Fetching up a heap of bric-a-brac
A particular history
Deeply embedded
Plenty potentially

Which if we could co-ordinate it
Would come across
As a record of small civilities
Some of which may be inadmissible
No attempt made
Where it says excessively
Like moving from one pocket to
another
In the street this morning
Continual change

iv.
You strike me as contemporary
I see you have all the attributes
Scuffed elbows and dirty toes
Subject to the say-so
As thought we might
Fold back in
Picked up I mean
Registered etc.
To seek and

I mean thus
As though we might
Establish in accordance
Some kind of fictive theatre
Maybe would startle it into life.
In the street the plum tree
And on the plum tree
Waxwings
At work early
And now they
Range.

v.
With the utmost degree of intensity
The tree opposite
Across a wooden table
Accumulating books
La Medusa by Vanessa Place
Dance Writings by Edwin Denby
The ones I can see
At least and the term
Contemporary
Clear and
Unequivocal

It won't be.
That much we know.
It is a moment of
Maximum visibility
The bitter wind searching eagerly
Houses for which I can vouch
But can't quite see
The tree opposite
Backed by sunlight
Considerably disturbed
Something has left
The language.

vi.
That tree again
Which the birds left
And now come back to
May suspend temporarily
Companions of the earth
As one might say
This first day of spring
Now it is backed by sunlight
Itself
Against the crosswires
Like Cy Twombly.

Calm in the assurance
An everyday frame of life
Suspended maybe
In its entirety
A blatant opening up
Witness that tree
This day of all days
Disclosing itself
Against the wires
March 5th 2013
Approximately
Normal.

vii.
I find other materials
Feeling for the whole arrangement
From Dover to Calais
Not even
The traffic stops
And you told me about it
So now I know
I am a credible witness
As then as there
The underlying structure contributes

Other materials
To be carried out and
Used directly
Just such necessary measures
Like the workings of the feet
As the evidence checks out
Whoso extends
This evening
Listen
No invented house
No imaginary site.

viii.
The simple thing to say is
The blackbird checks out
Set down on the white plane
Exactly where the public law stops
Something in the situation that would
Never have happened
I think to tell you that in change
Thought is made in the mouth.

The blackbird checks out
I assemble an elaborate voicemail
Made from work bricks and other materials
Employed to extend the sense of touch
Laths which
As such
May suspend temporarily
Like Twombly articulated by Agamben
Designated
Falling beauty

I go to designate the blackbird
He checks out without me noticing
I tell you
Using primarily
Strips of wood
Assemblages that extend
Bricks and other materials
Partial and incomplete
State movement
People

ix.
I walk away from the poem
It is an ok moment.
I'm like it's ok
And from the radio a quartet blares out
I guess
Though nobody says
I'm thinking it's an ok moment
Except for the echo
Which is strong
1827
Or thereabouts.

I work on the echo
I'm like ok ok
There are framing devices
That one day I'd like to tell you about
Witness context
A figure
In the transition between
And now I'm talking to the radio
This is not ok.

x.
I leave the following message
It is not ok
I speak with the implacability
Of the dead poet.
I call on Steve Collis of Vancouver
And my associates
The waxwings
Dear Jurisdiction –
Your conduct
Has become
Deplorable

I know it in my bones
It is past argument
I call on the trees and the
Street signs
As evidence
Echoing into place
A genuine and
Subsisting relationship
Here
Like houses
Shall comprise an area

xi.
May freely, safely
and without impediment
disturbance whatsoever
abide and trade
cross, stay
both by land and

any
and sea and
any
and may
and may

xii.
I write to you convinced
we shall comprise an area
it is a matter of holding
social space
open like a language
sometimes setting up camp
in the streets
the street signs
hammering
pots and pans

manufacturing an echo
something like
the evidence of intimacy
I write you through a language
remembering itself
partial and incomplete
across the noise which is
gathering
in the parks and
without impediment
keeping the powerful
awake

xiii.
I read into the night
Make notes on the new geography
Which is a series of interruptions
Partial and incomplete
And the waxwings that hold out
Making the analogy with collage
This evening in the lawscape
Only calm
Temporarily

Picked up in the street
The whole thing suspended in its entirety
Ensured in accordance
The everyday frame of life
This is my voicemail
I think we need other materials
Rectangular slabs
Bricks etc.

xiv.
Starting out
An observance
When a thyng is shapen
Something like
When the wind against
Sat down and made
A pull out map

On the common of No Man's Orchard
And many
Impartial
Duplicates
In the landscape
And then the wind
Drops

Old Town - New Story

PORTRAITS

ROBIN
GILLANDERS

"I wasn't really doing anything with my life until I got in contact with Crisis. As well as attending courses, I've now been offered a volunteer role helping out with the film club, which is a brilliant way to meet people and get involved with something worthwhile."

Crisis is a charity for single homeless people. Crisis Skylight Edinburgh works with single people who are homeless or vulnerably housed offering educational and work opportunities, one to one support and 'Crisis at Christmas'.

www.crisis.org.uk

Gary Walker, Crisis

"Canongate Youth is a saviour for our band, it is a place we can practice, a place we can make noise and not have someone telling us to turn it down!!! Ugh parents!!! And it has a studio, but most importantly it is a place where I have met nearly all of my current friends!!! "

"The staff are wonderful and experienced in music. They also give us many opportunities to play and get involved with organisations within old town Edinburgh and the general community."

Canongate Youth's vision is for children and young people to be healthy, happy and secure, belong in their communities and become confident and fulfilled adults.

www.canongateyouth.org.uk

Christy Logan, Sammy Harrison, Melissa Rozel, Canongate Youth Project

"Great Feats at Dance Base has helped me a lot with building up my confidence, also everybody is really nice. It's also situated in the Old Town of Edinburgh, which has great views of the castle and also is a really nice place to look around when you have some spare time."

Dance Base, Scotland's National Centre for Dance, is on a mission to get everyone dancing.

www.dancebase.co.uk

Nicole Gordon , Dance Base

"I came along to the café for a year or so before I started to organise the thrift shop on a Thursday, which I love doing. We don't charge a lot and all the money goes to Serenity. A huge cross-section of people come here and Serenity has really helped me to see things differently. I love the sociability and sense of community."

Comas has a clear social purpose, to improve the lives of everyone involved in their projects. Through the Serenity Café, people change their lives and find their passions and their potential, learning to live life to the full after mental illness, addiction or trauma.

www.serenitycafe.co.uk

Jane Matthews, Serenity Cafe

"Coming into the project gives me structure in my life and has boosted my confidence immensely. The Grassmarket is a thriving and exciting place and it thrills me to have the opportunity to come here and be part of it"

Grassmarket Community Project works among the most vulnerable of our citizens, helping people to reconnect firstly with themselves through increased self-esteem, secondly with others in a supportive environment and thirdly with the wider community through enterprise and training opportunities.

www.grassmarketcommunityproject.co.uk

Julie Tierney, Grassmarket Community Project

IN THE MONASTERY GARDEN

MORELLE SMITH

101

I could smell burning as soon as I came into the kitchen but I didn't have time to investigate before Daniel walked in from the back door. He went over to the coffee pot.

Ah no, he murmured, because he does not declaim and exaggerate, he does not call attention to himself and that, paradoxically, was the first thing about him that I noticed, not his height, though he is very tall, because there was very little of him to be seen. He was half way up a laurel tree at the time, camouflaged among the branches that he was pruning. It was only the whine of an electric saw and the shaking of the branches that located him at all. He looked a little fiercely at me but that's often the way with gardeners, and I put it down to him being interrupted in his work especially as it looked as if it was about to rain and he was making the most of the available time before the deluge. It was only later that I found out his history with this tree.

I was living in a former monastery, part of which has been converted into a writers' residence, in the French Alps. The view from my window looked out over the large garden, stepped into terraces, and onto the mountains beyond. When the monks lived here, they used to give produce from the garden to the villagers. I did not imagine, in early April, that there would be any produce but every day Daniel left some leeks and broccoli for us, which must have been planted, I supposed, the year before.

There was snow on the mountain tops and the trees were still bare. Everyone was talking about how late the spring was this year. Each morning I scrutinized the tree-covered mountain slopes and came to believe that there was a minute, ever so slight shift in colour, a lightening, a pale golden gleam coming off the trees like a faint lingering mist or a ray of sunlight reflected from some invisible shiny surface. The upper slopes of the village were festooned with trees beside the paths and in gardens. Only a few reckless buds were emerging around the ancient medieval walls and the damp-darkened facades of the houses.

Sunny weather finally came after days so wet that you listened to the water pouring off the roof and thundering on the metal chairs and tables outside and feared that this old building that had suffered from centuries of damp and decay might once again crumble under the assault of water. But with the sun's arrival the trees sprang into blossom as if some mighty hand that had held each bud closed had been suddenly released. Blossom and small leaves rushed out to taste the sunlight and warm air. And so did I, finding a place under the shade of the laurel tree to park my table and chair.

But after a few days of blue skies and warm sun, I came back from shopping in the nearby market town and discovered that Daniel had been pruning again. Only one or two forlorn branches of laurel were left.

But why did you do this I said, that's my shady place! It turned out that the laurel's roots were affecting the foundations of the building and Daniel wanted to cut it down completely.

Well, what am I to do he says, one person asks me this, another wants that, you will need to confer among yourselves, decide what you want. There are other places, you know, look, how about down there, by the bamboo, there's plenty of shade there. But by the bamboo, the earth is rough, uneven, and the line of bamboo, like a fence, makes me feel uneasy.

Or here, says Daniel. Further on and close to the wall, a little quince tree, solitary, tucked round a corner out of sight. I decide I like this tree, with one or two shrunken fruits from last year's crop just beginning to show a few flowers, faintly pink, an unobtrusive tree, whose nature I can warm to.

OK I say, but if you could just cut the grass beneath it a little bit....

And how might you like it cut, a circle, a rectangle, a square? A circle I suppose, for the energy?

Yes a circle would be....

No, there are people coming from the television on Thursday. I want to leave it as it is. Friday, I can cut it then.

If you have some shears I can cut it myself I say, but Daniel is adamant it should be left.

Thursday morning I am at my table beneath the quince tree and the television crew appears and talks to this one then to another one then to others who arrive to talk about this or that aspect of the monastery, historians, school teachers, administrators, local guides, local residents. When I meet Daniel coming down the steps with a daisy tucked behind his ear apologizing for the disruption of my peace, that is the final straw. I abandon my quince tree, put on my sun hat, pack a bottle of water, and go for a long walk up the old salt route that begins down in the valley just below the village. I walk a long way up the mountain, up to where there's a house that may be abandoned or maybe is only lived in during the summer months, and there's such a view out over the valley and such silence.

It is not a good day, Daniel said quietly but definitively, that was his pronouncement, when he saw that it was the handle of the miniature coffee pot that had fallen off, and was smouldering on the hot plate.

Don't be downcast I said, it's just a coffee pot and the smallest one at that, I will make you some coffee. He left the kitchen, carrying the two parts of the pot, lowering his head slightly as he went through the door.

Might have something to do with the laurel tree, I said to the empty doorway.

I made coffee in the medium sized pot and called to him when it was ready. He thanked me but still looked glum as he strode up the wide steps from the lower level of the garden. Perhaps there was something else weighing on his mind that he had not told me. Perhaps no gardener likes to be told how to run his garden. He and the laurel tree, they had history after all and I was a mere temporary resident, who had inadvertently come between him and the tree. He was the gardener, the one who knew. His authority had been undermined and his slicing of the branches was his way of reducing that tyranny little by little and all I wanted was some shade that was close enough to the building so that I did not have to carry a tray of things with me each time I went out.

The next day, walking down the wide steps towards my quince tree, I noticed on the outside shelf of the little window of the barn where the garden implements are kept, the pack of coffee and the two pieces of the small pot. Testament or evidence perhaps, yet they had the look of a bitter farewell note.

It's the weekend, the sunny days have fled and the clouds are snarling up in the mountains, threatening us with rain. I want Daniel to turn up on Monday morning, I want him to smile. I want to thank him for the vegetables he has left in the basket on the outside table for our use I want to tell him how good the poirots taste, how good the garden looks now, with its areas of dug earth, and already young lettuce plants growing in other strips, and how I appreciate his work and I am even ready to sacrifice the laurel tree because I know that as the gardener he knows best, and besides I have another tree now and besides, it's cloudy and the temperature has dropped and because of the abrupt change in the weather I have a head cold, and have barely stepped outside all week end.

If he comes back I will devise a plan to capture his attention. Perhaps I will make him coffee, offer lessons in English conversation, there's still time to think up something, still time.

POEMS

JOCK
STEIN

~~~

MIKE
SAUNDERS

~~~

ALAN
GILLIS

~~~

107

CLOUD AND FIRE

Surreal winter cloudscape, three times layered
along the Ochils, cradling Sherriffmuir
as if to gentle history, and make
an overture in art to things impossible.

Take time and outstretched fingers, run them
carefully along those bars of fog, soft striped
dawnwear for the hills which know the time
to sleep, and wake when Spring unfolds, to
do the duty of each season; or maybe
veils, concealing futures languishing
in jails, unvisited since unimagined?
What season now for Scotland, what videotype
of land is waiting to be brought to birth?
Stylish, connected, rich in mind — or just unkind?

What poet politician is there who will dare
lift off the blindfolds we all wear
and speak the words we cannot say?
What fire by night will match the cloud by day?

Jock Stein

REFERENDUM
April 2014

Our types are chosen: Ayrshire bard, Aberdeen
oilman, Ettrick shepherd, Falkirk bairn
for me, and maybe just a touch of Allan
Ramsay: 'On this brae I crack with kings'.

'Whit's for ye'll no go past ye.' Is that saw
our closest call with providence? What about
the Darien disaster, or the Royal Bank,
did they just happen? Are we dust or fleas
on Satan's hoof or can we claw back
some humanity, and choose with courage?
Who am I? What values cross my path, or
cross my palm and lead me to the dark side?

Give me mongrel strength. No bigsy breeding,
no wracked, cracked genes, feeding cringe
or needing binge of drunken make believe.
If we have myths, let them be kind and true,
to make us song and symbol, right and wrong,
so we can live and die for something strong.

Jock Stein

LIVE STREAM AURORA BOREALIS

To see it face north, away from areas of pollution
and when walking around the neighbourhood at dusk, a thin coat,
more luck will be had looking out over water
before the phone call the Norfolk reds were luminous with impatience —
so, here is everything you need to know
a sharp sickle moon buoyant,
the twin peaks patter of the solar maximum
unwild suburban light,
a mass ejection of particles from the sun
cold voices overlapping an atmospheric indifference.
the further north you are, the more likely it is you will see
And then it was never visible, and I was silent
a soft adventure
and you said, well, at least the blue dark is still here
we do not want to get too many people's hopes up only to see them dashed
and I said I can't see it, I just can't see it

Mike Saunders

DOCUMENT
March 2013

The grocer at the end of our street told me it would be a good idea
to eat two onions a day. He said it would really help my skin
and while I didn't really think there was any problem with   .
my skin in the first place, it seemed wise to follow his
suggestion. He made other suggestions, which
I realise I have ignored. I record myself
here for the idea of a portrait of
a specific place and taste of
that place, for the air
around the window
filled buzzing
with flies

without any of the reasons we are told flies
collect in a single place for, and for
this taste in my mouth, a little like
metal and acid and the bad part
of an onion, so that I or
someone else may
come back and
find my skin
improved
or worse

may come back to this space of
voices and text diminished
and remember or learn
something from the
structure of this
unspecific
moment.

Mike Saunders

SPRING

You might have butterflies
for no reason, all antsy
as if in anticipation
of the leaves' first look-and-see-me.

You might crack your nut trying to take in
the what of it, its here and this
while it lifts its skirts to brush by you,
streaming past with one light kiss.

Bare-knuckled sycamores start wearing green.
Cherry blossom froths and pirouettes
in a brook, trickling past these streets
and estates, sloshing beneath tarmac,

visible here, underground there, everywhere
guzzling as the narrow-banked brook
rushes past scraggy reeds and weed tufts,
cacked plastics, sewer scurf, beer-can stooks,

streaming along in the green-glinted leaf-swish
and ripple of a petal-scented zing,
and with it flows all that we know of the here-
it-comes and there-it-goes of everything.

Alan Gillis

GREEN ODES

Get off your arsehole son, the end is nigh.
You got high
on your hellfire, didn't you? Well tired of you
I walked until my feet screamed.
I walked until it seemed
one thing was always reflected in another,
all days interconnected. O mother
with the dong of a bell
in my ear I set out my own stall: if the end is near they can all
go to hell.

Ω

I'll write green odes, walking mean roads
with damaged feet, through ravaged wheat
fields drooled with pus, an unwheeled school bus
in a ditch, rabbits and birds
flitched to squirts and gizzards,
broken-hipped deer addled in the dirt,
their blackened lips queer with curdled yoghurt
under a red sky,
the rotten wind a hot pin
in the eye.

Alan Gillis

READING WAVERLEY BACKWARDS

STUART KELLY

There are many reasons why Sir Walter Scott's posthumous reputation declined so precipitously. He is wordy in an era in thrall to Hemingway's concision at one end of the aesthetic spectrum and Twitter at the other. He thinks a man can find his true self on the battlefield — an opinion that might have been true if one were talking about Flodden or Culloden or even Waterloo but looks naive and jingoistic after Ypres, Passchendaele and the Somme — let alone Stalingrad or Auschwitz. His female characters are sometimes characterised only by hair colour (not always, it should be said). His view of history as a constant amelioration strikes many as conservative, or lazy, or simplistic.

In his lifetime, he was thought the equal of Shakespeare, even by his detractors. By the end of the nineteenth century, writers as different as Mark Twain and Emile Zola were deriding him; modernists as different as Joyce and Forster would write patronisingly about him in the twentieth century; FR Leavis would exclude him from the "Great Tradition"; and in the 21st century contemporary writers in Scotland, for the most part, view him as either the embarrassing uncle best kept in the attic or as an actively malign defender of the British status quo and oppressor of more progressive voices. In the groves of academe, more subtle voices are beginning to re-appreciate Scott's nuance, slyness and ambiguity, but for the general reader, Scott is still a Dead White Tory Heterosexual Male Who Wrote Too Many Too Long Books. Worse still, Tony Blair chose Scott's *Ivanhoe* for his Desert Island Discs reading, long before he became Prime Minister. Could bellicosity, verbosity, casual sexism and a complacent belief in "progress" come together in any more perfect storm? No wonder you will find more copies of Scott in Oxfam than Waterstones.

The bicentenary of his first novel, ought to be a time to re-evaluate Scott's importance and — whisper it — his radicalism.

One of the principal reasons for the neglect of Scott is that we insist on reading him backwards. Scott is seen as the precursor to the great Victorian novelists — to Dickens in terms of humour, to the Brontës in terms of pathetic fallacy, to Hardy in terms of tragedy, to Eliot in terms of social insight (let alone Balzac), to Fenimore Cooper, Bulwer-Lytton and Harrison Ainsworth in terms of rollicking plot (let alone Dumas), to Stevenson in terms of dissecting national identity (let alone Tolstoy). He is read as a step towards such writers, and found wanting in terms of not having stepped sufficiently far. This is a misguided approach to Scott's work. Born in 1771, Scott's roots, intellectually and aesthetically, are in the eighteenth century. If one reads Scott as a writer continuing the experiments and advances of the eighteenth century — as the heir to Fielding, Swift, Smollett and Sterne, the descendant of Burney, Radcliffe, Mackenzie and Reeve — he makes far more sense as a writer. Furthermore, as a man formed by the Scottish Enlightenment, a reading of Scott which puts him in the context of Adam Smith's moral empathy, David Hume's scepticism, William Robertson's historiography, Adam Ferguson's sociology and Hugh Blair's aesthetics, reveals him as a novelist of uncommon intellectual engagement. For all that E M Forster might dismiss Scott's work with the lines "Who shall tell us a story? Why, Walter Scott of course", there is significantly more to his work that the mere pleasures of unfolding narrative.

The opening pages of *Waverley* make this abundantly clear. The first chapter of *Waverley* begins with wondering what kind of novel *Waverley* might have been, had its subtitle — " or 'Tis Sixty Years Since" — been different. The omniscient narrator (Scott's most overlooked character in some ways) riffs on alternative *Waverleys*. There is a gothic *Waverley* (a Tale of other Days), full of crypts and keeps and secrets. There is *Waverley* — "a Romance from the German" — which we might now recognise as a Dan Brown style thriller ("a secret and mysterious association of Rosycrucians and Illuminati, with all their properties of black cowls, caverns, daggers, electrical machines, trap-doors and dark-lanterns"). There is *Waverley* — A Sentimental Tale, featuring a maiden playing the harp and a "blowsy peasant girl whose jargon [the heroine] can hardly understand", and *Waverley* — A Tale of the Times, full of "dashing sketches" and "private scandal thinly veiled". This is clearly influenced by Sterne's self-consciousness about the novel, but, despite the tentative nature of the introduction, there is a more serious point that Scott is making; as the *Waverley* we are holding includes all these hypothetical *Waverleys* and much more. Scott satirises the gothic novel's ruined halls and jocular valets — but includes down-at-heel aristocratic piles and in Davie Gellatley, an "innocent" clown whose pronouncements undercut the more romantic hyperbole. It is a novel that depends upon conspiracies, and Edward Waverley will meet his fair share of dirks and caves along the way. In Chapter XXII, we read that "Here, like one of those lovely forms which decorate the landscapes of Poussin, Waverley found Flora gazing on the waterfall. Two paces further back stood Cathleen, holding a small Scottish harp, the use of which had been taught to Flora by Rory Dall, one of the last harpers of the Western Highlands", the very scene the opening told us would not occur — and characters will speak in both Scots and Gaelic. And as a Tale of the Times? The final chapter, with the witty title of "A Postscript Which Should Have Been A Preface", Scott reflects on how the events of the narrative have conditioned the contemporary political and socioeconomic situation. Were one to wish for some "private scandal thinly veiled", then in the Magnum Opus edition released towards the end of Scott's life, he lays bare the family history concerning Jacobitism which informed his portrayal of the rebellion. This is also — though few readers at the time would link the biographical facts to the literary fiction — the story of a man who convinced himself to take second-best: Scott, even after his wife's death, would write about the heartbreak of losing the girl he first loved.

Waverley's opening caper of metafictional sprezzatura might be read as a tyro novelist's lack of confidence. But this underestimates one of Scott's most profound insights as a novelist: that the novel is essentially and importantly a hybrid form, a strangely capacious and generous come-all-ye. What *genre* is *Waverley*? It is a historical novel, some might say. Novels had, however, been set in the past before; but *Waverley* included real people alongside fictional creations, and showed how both might be caught up in the tides and torrents of "history", not just events. It is a romance — Edward Waverley ends happily married, and Scott is astute in rendering the psychology of mature love growing out of blustering infatuation. It is a satire, with the shadow of Don Quixote falling over Waverley's predisposition to prefer fantasy and chivalry to reality and bloodshed. It is a tragedy, with Waverley's one-time prospective brother-in-law going to the gallows, and his loyal, feudal servant following him: more than that, Waverley's first love gets the novel's most impressive and poignant speech — "'I do not regret his attempt because it was wrong! — O no! on that point I am armed — but because it was impossible it could end otherwise than thus". (The word "impossible", incidentally, is scattered throughout *Waverley* - twenty-seven occurrences according to Project Gutenberg. Characters are perpetually denying what they are doing is real, or questioning whether mere prose can reflect experience).

Waverley is not so much a novel, as a sampler of what novels can choose to do. When one looks at the other works Scott published in the same year, this is less surprising. 1814 saw the publication of Scott's edition of the works of Jonathan Swift: he had spent the past few years pondering such unclassifiable books as *The Tale Of A Tub* and *Gulliver's Travels* (or, to give it its actual title *Travels into Several Remote Nations of the World. In Four Parts. By Lemuel Gulliver, First a Surgeon, and then a Captain of Several Ships*). It was also the year he published a review of the Highland Society's enquiry into the authenticity of James Macpherson's "Ossian" poems. In a judicious and open-minded essay, Scott wrestled with the fact that Scotland's most significant contribution to European culture in the past two centuries was not as "real" as it had been taken to be: might there be a way to write about Scotland, genuinely, encompassing both Gaelic relics and "modernist" philosophy, without resorting to imposture? That his first novel would appear anonymously seems comprehensible with these links: Swift did not "author" his book, nor did Macpherson. *Waverley*, famously, had no author on its title page.

He also wrote, but did not publish, a diary of his tour around Scotland's lighthouses. In it, we see the Scott who is deeply suspicious of literature, not just wary: "It would be a fine situation to compose an ode to the Genius of Sumburgh Head, or an Elegy on a Cormorant or to have written or spoken madness of any kind in prose of poetry. But I gave vent to my feelings in a more simple way; and sitting gentle down on the steep green slope which lead to the beach, I e'en slid down a few hundred feet, and found the exercise quite an adequate vent to my enthusiasm, I recommend this exercise (time and place suiting) to all my brother scribblers, and I have no doubt it will save much effusion of Christian ink".

Yet there is an author referred to very early on in *Waverley*. Before we read Scott's joshing, serious account of the genesis of the book, there is the title page and its epigraph: "Under which King, Bezonian? Speak or die" — a line from Shakespeare's *Henry IV Part II*. A bezonian might mean either a new recruit or a rascal, a beggar, a knave. (The word occurs again in the same play: "Great men oft die by vilde Besonions"). On one hand the reader is invited to take this as a hint to the novel's themes. Will this be a book about treachery or naivety; criminals or innocents? At the same time, it is also a sly intervention from Scott, to Scott. Is he the new recruit, the untested lance in the field of prose fiction? Or is he an upstart crow, attempting things a wise man would know better than to do, purely for gain? Is the new unknown "Author of Waverley" killing off the "great man", Scott the poet, who had been offered the laureateship not long beforehand? Or is the shy, cautious Scott telling himself he knows this is a new field, a new departure, for his creative work?

That the quote is from Shakespeare is just as telling. Though we might now wince at critics claiming a writer is on a par with Shakespeare, there is no doubting that Scott has a Shakespearean quality. Much of this is filtered through German interpretations of Shakespeare — and Scott started his career translating such writers as Schiller and Goethe. What they found in Shakespeare, Scott included in his own work. He has the same range over class — the clown and king, the peasant and the prince, the lowly and the lordly. He has the same sense that tragedy and comedy are inextricably linked, and that history shows us both and neither. His greatest lines are all dialogue, not prose exposition; and his erudition and wit are lightly worn and deeply subtle.

One question troubles me whenever I think of Scott. Who nowadays attempts a novel of such inclusion, such diversity, such geographical and historical range? Scott's exclusion from the story of the novel has impoverished it, and he remains a resource that we might yet tap, and from which we might derive inspiration. Who else, after all, gave uncaricatured versions of the poor, the insane, the wrongfully convicted, Jews, Muslims, and Hindus? Who else in the nineteenth century showed us that our enemies and those whom we fear were human?

$$\frac{3}{3 \quad 6 \quad 5}$$

JAMES
ROBERTSON

1. VARIETIES OF MADNESS IN FRANCE, 1665
after Sir John Lauder

One night we happened to discourse on madmen and the causes of madness. They told me of a man at Marseilles who believed himself the greatest king of the world, and that all the ships in the harbour, along with their wares, were his. Of another they said that he believed himself to be made of glass, and cried horridly if anyone came too close, for fear they would break him. His friends, on some doctor's advice, took a great sandglass and smashed it over his head as he thus raged. When he saw the glass falling at his feet he cried more hideously than ever, that his head was broken in pieces. After he had calmed a little they desired him to consider that the glass was broken, but that he was not; and consequently that he was not glass. On this remonstrance he came to himself, admitting the truth of what they said.

We cannot forget a story from the bedlam in Paris. Two gentlemen came out of curiosity to see the madmen, but the keeper of the hospital having some business to attend could not take them round. Whereupon he instructed one of the inmates to accompany them, and show them all the madmen and the natures of their madness. This the man did, pointing out with remarkable knowledge one who was mad for love, another made witless through drunkenness, a third who was hypochondriac and so on. At last as they were about to leave the inmate said, 'Gentlemen, you have marvelled at the folly of many you have seen, but yonder is one more foolish than all the others, for that poor fellow believes himself to be the beloved apostle Saint John. Now I tell you that he is utterly wrong, and the reason I know this is that I am Saint Peter, and I never opened the gate of Heaven to him yet.'

The gentlemen were surprised to find their guide, so credible until that moment, so deeply deluded. They were informed that he was once a doctor in the college of Sorbonne, and had been reduced to that state through too much study. Which is a lesson indeed.

James Robertson

2. WAYS OF DYING GENTLY IN SCOTLAND, 1790s
after Lord Cockburn

Dr Joseph Black, the noted scientist, was a tall, thin, cadaverously pale person, feeble, slender and elegant; his eyes were dark, clear and large, like deep pools of water. He glided like a spirit through the mischief and sport of local boys, respected and unharmed; and when he died, seated with a bowl of milk on his knee, in ceasing to live he did not spill a drop of it.

Dr Robert Henry the historian, having been declining for some while, wrote from his Stirlingshire home to his friend Sir Harry Moncrieff: 'Come out here directly. I have got something to do this week, I have got to die.' Sir Harry arrived. Dr Henry was alone with his wife, resigned yet cheerful. Sir Harry stayed with them three days, during which Dr Henry occupied his easy chair, conversed, was read to, and dozed.

At one point, hearing the clattering of a horse's hooves in the court below, Mrs Henry looked out. To her dismay she saw that it was a wearisome neighbour, a minister, who was famous for never leaving a house after he once got into it. 'Keep him oot,' cried Dr Henry, himself a minister, 'don't let the cratur in here.' But already the cratur was up the stair and at the door. The doctor winked and signed to the others to sit still, while he pretended to be asleep. The visitor entered. Sir Harry and Mrs Henry put their fingers to their lips and shook their heads: the slumberer was not to be disturbed. The visitor took a seat, to wait till the nap should be over. Whenever he tried to speak, he was instantly silenced by another finger on the lip and another shake of the head. This continued for a quarter of an hour, with Sir Harry occasionally detecting his friend peeping through the fringes of his eyelids to check on the state of play. At last the unwanted guest was ushered out, at which the dying man opened his eyes and had a tolerably hearty laugh. This was followed by another when the sound of departing hooves assured them that the danger was past. Dr Henry died that night.

James Robertson

3. SCOTTISH DIETARY PREJUDICES
after Sir John Lauder and John Kay's Original Portraits

Sir John Lauder, on his travels in France in the 1660s, was not a little amazed to see his hosts one day preparing among other things for the daily meal 'upright puddock stools', which they called potirons or champignons. They rose overnight, he noted, and grew in 'humid, moisty places' as in Scotland. The French fried them in a pan with butter, vinegar, salt and spice, and ate them greedily, surprised that he did not eat as heartily of them as they did. 'But my prejudice hindered me,' Lauder rather ruefully admitted.

More than a century later, Dr Joseph Black and his friend Dr James Hutton, in the service of free and objective inquiry, set out to overturn a similarly narrow dietary prejudice. It was surely inconsistent, they argued, to abstain from the consumption of hard-shelled creatures of the land, while those of the sea were considered delicacies. If oysters, why not snails, for instance? Snails were known to be nutritious, wholesome and even to have healing properties. The Italians, like the epicures of antiquity, held them in high esteem. The two philosophers resolved to expose the absurd objections of their countrymen to the eating of snails.

Having procured a quantity, they caused them to be stewed for dinner. No guests were invited to the banquet. The snails were served – but theory and practice were found to be separated by a great gulf. Far from exciting their appetites, the smoking dish had diametrically the opposite effect, and neither party felt much inclination to partake of it. Disgusted though they both were by the snails, however, each retained his awe for the other; and so began with infinite exertion to swallow, in very small quantities, the mess that was prompting involuntary internal symptoms of revolt.

Dr Black at length delicately broke the ice, as if to sound the opinion of his companion. 'Doctor,' he said, in his precise and quiet manner, 'Doctor, do you not think that they taste a little – a very little queer?' 'Damned queer! Damned queer, indeed!' Dr Hutton at once responded. 'Tak them awa, tak them awa!' And, starting up from the table, he gave full vent to his feelings of abhorrence.

James Robertson

LETTER FROM VENICE

DAVID TOMASSINI

Back in Venice for the first time in a year, after having lived here for almost a decade, the young faces are familiar but I don't recognise anyone. That's because in the unending flow of pedestrians in the narrow streets, I am looking for faces as they were thirty years ago, when I first came. Not that my aging friends have changed that much, but there are fewer of them. Deaths and the steady haemorrhage of the resident population have taken their toll. The figures are incontrovertible. Over the last thirty years residents have been abandoning the historic centre of Venice at the rate of almost 1,000 a year (pop. around 80,00 in 1980, it was 56,741 in April 2014). Most have left for the same reason as I did. For the price of a small two-room flat in Venice you can buy a house to do up in the country. So who struggles on with the high tides and tourists? The rich and the relatively poor. Paradoxically, in proportionate terms, Venice has the largest number of council houses in any Italian city centre (social housing elsewhere has been pushed out to the periphery). It's the ever-growing lower middle classes — increasingly impoverished by the enduring deep general economic crisis — who are forced out. That means teachers, joiners, ironmongers, genuine booksellers, artists, grocers, non-tourist shopkeepers, lab technicians, office workers ... the normal sap of city life. The cinemas have all closed (there were five in 1985).

I run into my friend Annalisa, who has just picked up her granddaughter from nursery school. The kids are running freely all over the place while parents chat. I made great friends when my son was at nursery school. I'm still in touch with them but now they live in Trieste, Rome or in the country outside Mestre (mainland Venice) — the housing bleed. What makes Venetian nursery schools special is — to use a verbatim Italian translation — that they are 'interclassist'. Everyone sends their kids to the same school, from the consultant to the unemployed port worker, and pays accordingly. None of the odious British class divisions created by private schooling. Another special feature is that in this original 'urban village' everybody has to walk home after school so there are great discussions. Criticism, projects and plans for school in an informal way ... it fosters community spirit. Leaving aside the tourists, Venice has arguably the best urban quality in the world. It is pure city with a unique social dimension due to the total absence of the motor car. But now the critical mass of the creative city is dwindling towards extinction.

I'm staying with my old pal Antonio, a Calabrian who has been teaching economics in high school for thirty years. The southerners fit in well in Venice — Naples of the north — which has all the endearing features of the so-called 'lazy' south; unlike most of the rest of the North East which is stressed by efficiency and confused by creeping racism. Antonio rents a flat which he can only afford by subletting rooms. He's a bit of an artist too — photography and painting. He was greatly encouraged in this by a socially driven project involving the much feared and maligned *centri sociali*. These 'social centres' are kinds of self-managed meeting places often in 'occupied' disused buildings and found in most Italian cities. Run and/or used by anarchical and *movimento no-global* young people, they spontaneously set out to forge a different culture. You find all sorts, from drug abusers to revolutionaries, but I'm always struck about how more coherent they are politically than the historic hippies, because they actually pursue projects (community work, street markets, organic food, crafts, etc.) for developing and using the local area and so oppose the continuing culture degeneration (this is the land of Berlusconi but also Gramsci — the true struggle is for 'cultural hegemony'). In this particular case they took over the large 19th-century greenhouses that once belonged to the gardens where the Venice Architecture Biennale is now held. They did them up and made use of them. My friend Antonio initially got involved by chance after taking some photos of the very atmospheric old structure and then organising art shows. A committee was formed which eventually also negotiated with the city council and, after some resistance, they were given the required permits — and even some promotion. Run by a non-profit cooperative, the structure has partly been returned to its original function as a greenhouse by selling plants to the locals but with all sorts of other educational and cultural activities plus a bar (www.serradeigiardini.org). This example of participative social architecture stands in the shadow of what is probably at times the most futile big money 'starchitects' show worldwide (the Biennale). Antonio went on to develop his talent further with other shows, websites etc. What took him there was a spontaneous community project given a minimum of local government support.

I unconsciously skip round the incredibly still quiet backstreets — another unique feature of Venice is that if you think about street names you get lost, you just have to go on automatic pilot — to look up my friend Riccardo, a lecturer at Ca' Foscari University. He's in a glum mood over the latest proposals to put some of the university's finest *palazzi* up for sale. Buildings full of history such as Ca' Cappello on the Grand Canal, Ca' Bembo and Palazzo Cosulich. This move to 'modernise' the university (i.e. raise money to cover cuts) is certainly not going to be made without a fight. Students and lecturers have formed committees, one of the buildings has been occupied and the battle is still ongoing, also pending the appointment of a new rector (university rectors are powerful in Italy). The biggest criticism of the outgoing rector, who has also undeniably been very successful (Ca' Foscari is now one of the top three unis in Italy), is that he failed to involve staff and students in decisions.

I also learn about an even more shocking proposal: to create a 'Veniceland' in Venice. And the university to its — this time unequivocal — shame is also involved. An 80 million euro project for a theme park (ostensibly a virtual history museum with 'hyper reality workshops' but also fun fair complete with panoramic wheel) on the island of Sacca San Biagio, formerly the site of the city incinerator. The initial 400,000 annual visitor figure is expected to rise to 800,000 in 5-6 years. A drop in the ocean compared to the 25 million who visit Venice every year. So why bother? Because it will make the same kind of money for the entrepreneur behind the proposal, Alberto Zamperla, as it did for his 'Amusement Rides Company' (*sic*, as their slogan runs) in Eurodisneyland and more recently Coney Island. The company is a giant in the worldwide amusement parks business. Of course there is a carrot: 500 jobs; 'also for students at the nearby Ca' Foscari', we are assured — wouldn't it be better to leave them to their studies with suitable funding? Veniceland will more likely be staffed by the underpaid global workforce of immigrants and displaced persons. In terms of the struggle for cultural hegemony, the truly alarming fact is that the university is collaborating in this project in the form of the 'Ca' Foscari Foundation', set up with Zamperla to 'strengthen, make the most of and develop the university's activities'. This is more state property being sold off to raise cash. The locals have alternative projects but no financial clout ... the same old story. Why not build it in nearby depressed Marghera and Mestre? — plenty of post-industrial waste grounds just waiting to be redeveloped there. And you have lots of space to park the buses. Why should Zamperla get an easy share of the 25 million visitors?

San Biagio is not the only endangered island. Over the past few decades Venice has been selling off its islands (some former quarantine hospitals or mental asylums) in the name of tourism at any cost (San Clemente, Santa Maria delle Grazie and Sacca Sessola — the only exception is San Servolo — run by the province as a residential conference centre and an international university). Now it's the turn of Poveglia, an historic island off Malamocco (at the end of the Lido). But residents citywide are putting up a fight and have formed a subscription committee ('Poveglia for Everyone': www.facebook.com/povegliapertutti) to raise money and try and buy the island. Selling off islands is familiar story for Scottish readers and there are many similarities (Venice is even going to have a referendum on 'independence' for the historic centre — too complicated and paradoxical to tackle here). In the event a Venetian entrepreneur won the auction and even pledged to make public use of the island, possibly due to the influence of the committee. The ridiculous thing was that the quality of the projects was not considered, or only marginally, and the island was simply auctioned off to the highest bidder. The actual offer (600,000 euros) was so low, however, that the state land agency changed its mind and now the whole process has been stalled by legal wrangling. Whatever the outcome, the committee itself must be seen as a success and the Venetians' growing awareness of their rights and willingness to fight for their city.

On the subject of islands there is one example of good practice, however. On the islands of Mazzorbo and Sant'Erasmo, two enlightened entrepreneurs (Gianluca Bisol and Michel Thoulouze, a founder of pay TV in Europe) have invested in renewing local agriculture and redeveloping historic vineyards with attendant employment prospects in an eco-sustainable way on publicly-owned land (historically Sant'Erasmo is the 'garden of Venice' supplying the Rialto market).

With all these ongoing new battles I almost forgot to mention 'Moses' or *Mose* as the colossal eyesore of a barrier to keep out the *acqua alta* (high tide flooding) is called. Along with the tourist tides, *acqua alta* is Venice's biggest problem. So far Moses has divided the people more than the waters. Even Edinburgh trams pale in comparison with the timescale and rising costs of the *Modulo Sperimentale Elettromeccanico* — Electromechanical Experimental (sic) Module: the estimated cost in 2001 of 1.8 billion euros soared to 5.5 billion by 2013. While many alternative (though equally 'experimental') proposals for several more eco-sustainable micro-interventions at a fraction of the cost were made, they could not compete with the self-aggrandizement (and huge kickbacks) of the 'epoch-making great works' of the Berlusconian age (shades of the kind 'heroic, all of a piece schemes' that Patrick Geddes fought against in favour of 'primary human needs'). Local government only put up a fairly passive resistance. The mayor in office at the time, Massimo Cacciari, a philosophy professor and once the darling of the radical chic, gave a decidedly ancient regime riposte that would have pleased Billy Connolly: 'Let them wear wellies' (Cacciari even bears a passing resemblance to Geddes — the similarity stops there). A bit difficult to put wellies on bags of flour in storerooms. But the technocrats and politicians were given almost unlimited 'special' powers to meet the 'emergency' (the phenomenon of *acqua alta* has existed as long as Venice, only now it is more frequent probably due to the deep water channels for the port created in the 1960s and global warming). Although the ordinary citizens can hardly be expected to enter the 'scientific' debate about whether Mose will work when it eventually swings into action, probably next year, or how harmful the effects will be on the lagoon ecosystem, they might have been offered different choices than simply trusting the blind queen technology and her handmaidens of corruption (the first arrests have already been made across all political parties, the mayor has been forced to resign, and the scandal is taking on the dimensions of the notorious Milanese *tangentopoli* — "bribeville"— of the early 1990s). In the days of the doges even 'lowly' fishermen were consulted on questions affecting them. The court is still out on Moses but most of the locals feel little was done to explore alternatives and make better use of the money.

So here too the story is the same: not enough participative democracy involving all stakeholders and especially residents (it's they who have to put with the *acqua alta*). And yet Italy boasts some of the most innovative approaches to democratic urban planning, such as Alberto Magnaghi's 'territorialist' theories and projects in Tuscany. Thankfully many of the remaining Venetian residents are not giving up without a fight and their ideas and awareness may well be of interest to people in similar struggles elsewhere.

'Save Venice' is the name of a very active noble, American-run charity dedicated to preserving the artistic heritage of the city and restoring its churches. To 'save the Venetians', on the other hand, the national and local authorities must not simply yield to market logic. More farsighted and enlightened forms of government — and what better example than Venice's own historic Grand Council with its careful, thorough regulation of the public interest — are possible. The way forward is surely to empower resourceful residents who wish to build a sustainable future for themselves and a city that is not only unique in terms of its architecture but arguably also for its grass roots culture and community life.

MARIO RELICH

CHRISTINE DE LUCA

SAMANTHA WALTON

133

ART CRITIC

It was in 1945, not long
after the war, that I first
revelled in Paul Klee:
His paintings on show

in the National Gallery,
I saw daylight streaming
from the windows,
heralding the end

of sirens and air-raids.
But lately, honoured
by seventeen
claustrophobic rooms

for the exhibition
at the Tate Modern,
something of their colour-
coded vibrancy captured

in my memory was lost.
Yet *Like a Window Pane*,
far from dulled, was
dazzling in its dripping

squares of shimmering
colour. It looked like
an abstract pattern
on stained glass

in a modern cathedral.
Just gauze on cardboard,
but so translucent,
it still made its impact.

A poet as well, he
was much better
known for his
luminous prose,

as in *Pedagogical
Sketchbook*,
where he takes
a *line for a walk*.

The 1945 exhibition
I remember is to-day
long-forgotten, but
a year later, Orwell

wrote: *Good prose
is like a window pane.*
Klee's art makes us note
how poetic that sounds.

Mario Relich

STILL BEING
Heron in the Botanics

I love your oneness with a restless world,
your contentment with a proferred habitat:
embodied concentration, each synapse static,
while I barely linger long enough to focus.

Today you seek the susurrus of stillness:
the Chinese Garden with its seemly pond.
You don't do scruffy chic or informality:
each feather knows its place. Even this

arctic draught can't undo your poise,
your studied nonchalance; the grace in
your reflected image, a hunched perfection,
stuff of metaphor. When, with a coyness,

a moorhen dips her red dab in the pool,
twitches and birls, you still steadfastly
refuse to blink; still gaze into a quandary
of reeds, a contemplation of bamboo.

The ducks spook you. Like me, you move off,
gingering your way as if hidden landmines lay
in your path; each tiptoe hazarding dismay,
each step a testing of tentative truth.

Christine De Luca

I DY STRIDE

for Ana Maria Maguire, based on the statue of
the poet Robert Fergusson, Canongate, Edinburgh

Prunk in bronze, du's stendin doon   well set up; you're striding
da Canongaet, cott tails flaagin.   flapping loosely
Naeboady wid jalouse a Bedlam endin.   suspect; local mental asylum

Touries daander up ta dee, pose   tourists, wander, you
for der pictir. Du sood hae a page   You should have
in Facebook. Maybe du dis.   you do

Ee lass cups dy shin ithin her haands   One girl, chin
while her laad snaps her; anidder een   boyfriend, another one
claps dy cheek; dey sheeks wi dee,   strokes your, blether

der wirds catcht on camera.   caught
Anidder wife, for her album, harks   Another, whispers
i dy lug; hit's on her mobile, nae doot   in your ear, no doubt

half-gaets roond da wirld bi noo.   half-way, now
A man tries to place his feet
in exactly dy step; tooms up, snap,   thumbs

snap again. Some lean fornenst dee,   against
pit a airm aroond dee. A bairn plunks   put an arm,
her saaft toy, her peerie dug, i da crook   dog

o dy airm. Click. Hit's lik as if du's   of your arm. It's as if you are
faider, lover, pal. Ee halliget lass loups   One unrestrained girl leaps
apö dy back. Wir faert shö'll rive dy cott,   on, We're afraid she'll tear your coat

boofel dee. But du's mair bördly   pummel you, more robust
as du luiks. Stend on, man. Wir still   than you look. Stride, we're
staandin apö dy shooders, dy wirds.   on your shoulders, your words

Christine De Luca

SEALOCK

My steel heart is broken,
but I have veins into the valleys.
Soap bottles clog my
burning mouth
but the silt I smelt is under your head,
is the groove
of your most immediate and earliest
bedrock.

I cross asphalt, at dusk, to find you.
I brave white lines soaring under me
and the way my eyes stream,
hydrocracker, I can always see you
by the lights of your spine, lucent under
the horizon, the curve of earth
is the hand you cup,
is the love you syphon.

We've grown together,
not travelled, but seen flashes ascend,
touched another land like the hope
of the huff of delirium.
Our stale sweat tender and entrenched
is conquering, like nerves,
the nation.

We're out of touch
of flares tonight, sated by each other's breath
& bristling from the intimacy of a true north sky.
This town is a dead weight,
but not a burden.
The highstreet is alight, & houses hug

the ground they grew from.
We are piped into privacy
and sunk by the carbon
we maintain, two hopeless lovers
bruising the frozen pitch,
shattering shutters.
Every bus shelter here is
petrified exodus.

Swinging our legs over the
geometric un-shore
grazing our nylons in the shallow wake
we turn up ships like old peat soldiers
ash for eyes, ash lungs,
freight sunk by hub artery,
commodity fresh but
blood-adhesive
rock-oil.

Our raft of the Medusa exit strategy
is drunk in sulfur,
sulfur never to be admired fire spears
efflorescent in upturned antique skies,
enjoined to raze plains, or
cosseted in neat script,
recipes for purification
held close to the chestplate in the
cherished and salt-splattered
Libor Ignium, Book of Fires.

The earthwork is still high,
our defensive sod and clot,
the berm we sink into, our scrap
elbows consumed by, not piercing,
the protective wall of shame.
In the distance, the cooling towers of the free zone turn up dust
while the mirage of the Ochils
shimmers
purple and blue slate.
Our cat's cradle geographies
are becoming more refined, airborne ideas woven into
the fabric of the glow, silent but catalytic.
In our post-union attic,
crude romance flares unhinged
with the all-night show ended
polyester curtains hum orange.

Samantha Walton

COFFEE IS IT

TODD McEWEN

What do you think Edinburgh used to smell of? At various periods it has smelled of horse shit, human poo, wood smoke, coal smoke, tobacco smoke, Brasso, fish, gunpowder, flowers, ink, books and blood. When I came to live here it always smelled of boiling hops, especially in the Canongate. Sometimes people used to be able to smell the freshness of the Forth and even, they say, the yellow broom on the hills of Fife.

Now it smells of coffee, and coffee alone. Not even tea! Tea is dead. *Tea— dead*, in Edinburgh. Think. That must mean that all the Morningside ladies in pretty hats have died, along with all the railway workers in dungarees and bandannas. Who has replaced them? I will tell you: Alien Beings. Coffee is the fluid exuded by the nasty, half-fleshy, half-mechanical probes of these Beings, the Marketers from Outer Space, who came in their coffee bean pods and have taken over our city.

The first thing they did was make a tunnel. Aliens always do that. They bored a tunnel from the Royal Scottish Academy to the National Gallery. This 'space', as they call it, was created in order to sell coffee, because no one cares about art any more and you have to use the buildings for something!

The tunnel drips with the dark brown slime of capitalism. The other day I followed an old couple around — the kind of old couple you see around the galleries, all dry-cleaned and not speaking to each other even though they have rosy cheeks. They had coffee at the National Gallery, the City Art Centre and the National Museum and they never looked at a picture. Because they were *stoned*. On coffee.

CROWS.

Coffee is the tool by which the Marketers have turned our hallowed institutions into our hollow institutions.

The National Gallery's web site is full of crowing. It crows that the 'Gardens Entrance' (the tunnel of slime) 'offers spectacular views over Princes Street Gardens'. It does not. The windows are obscured with garish painted-on signs advertising coffee. As if to bolster this crassness, large A-boards advertising coffee have been placed in the Gardens for us to stumble over. As if you couldn't see the gigantic lettering in the windows of the restaurant, or you laughably and miserably and mistakenly assumed that here was a large public building in Edinburgh where you *couldn't* buy coffee. These A-boards are now stumbled and fallen over in front of every god damn business in our city. But they are not merely stumble-boards. *They are the egg-cases of the Marketers.*

GUNNERA.

The Marketers from Outer Space have laid many eggs in the Royal Botanic Garden. Here the soil is most conducive to their reproductive milt. This will be obvious to any observant citizen, as every time one visits the Garden there is less plant matter and more SIGNAGE. These signs are now an organism unto themselves, self-fertilizing and generating, having been grafted with the prolific and hideous *Gunnera manicata* near the East Gate. The signage organism is sentient and is planning to take over the entire Garden, if not the whole of our city. Several months ago, large signboards announcing a temporary closure of the glasshouses *erected themselves* overnight.

Sometimes the signage uses ideograms of people peeing, or buying something, or cups of coffee. Sometimes the signs eat children.

The Garden, in its wisdom (botanists on the board of directors already replaced by Marketer pod-people) built a galumphing new facade at the west side, the 'Gateway of Faint Hope'. This frightening structure was stated to be for 'educational purposes', the same dishonest reason given by the Gallery pod-people for their slime-cavern. But 'museum education' is just marketing. The main purpose of the Gateway is to sell coffee, which was already being sold by the gallon just a *few metres* away.

ARSE QUARTER.

The Marketers have determined that culture must be contained — it is a threat to them, after all. Therefore we must have an 'arts quarter'. This used to be called Grindlay Street. The arrival of the idea of the arts quarter was signalled by the appearance of a terrifying glass goitre on the side of the Usher Hall. No, not a goiter — since the Usher Hall used to be a place of mentation and pleasure, let's say a tumour, *literally a brain tumour on the left temporal lobe of the Usher Hall*, a sober but previously considerable Beaux-Arts building. The purpose of this goitre or tumour is the vending of coffee.

The Royal Lyceum theatre suffered a similar internal haemorrhage; the Traverse, medico-historically speaking, succumbed to coffee long ago; it is said to float on an underground lake of it. What untold riches!

MACCHIATO: THE SMELL OF FEAR.

The National Library smells not of morocco, which is to say of literature, but of cappuccino, which is to say of money. And money is the smell of hubris. They've put out wanky metal tables on the sidewalk on George IV Bridge, to stumble over, and where scholars may cool their lattes at most times of the year and attempt to smoke in the gale. (Since we're ruining our city, o Marketers, what happened to smoking? It's just as bad for you as coffee and vodka — for quite a while in its history Edinburgh smelled like one big wet Craven "A" — yet it gets short shrift now.)

The whole building, the entire national collection, and, by extension, *the totality of our cultural heritage, in every venue, now reeks of arabica.*

NEWTONIAN GAGGIA MECHANICS.

The upper galleries at Modern Two are located directly above the giant coffee machine in the shape of Isaac Newton on the ground floor (one of the largest espresso machines in the shape of a polymath bending over ever constructed in the former United Kingdom) so that you cannot think about art (even though it's usually only Paolozzi), but are instead driven to distraction by the rank fumes of burning coffee and the thought maybe of one of those little polenta cakes. These rooms are obscured in a haar of espresso.

PARTY!

There is one odour of present-day Edinburgh that can (briefly) come out on top of coffee, and that is the smell of a stag night. They let these things happen in the Grassmarket, because A: the city fathers, their bodies and spinal cords inhabited by the alien marketers, have given up on the Old Town, and B: the city fathers think the smell of a stag night can be contained there. On any Thursday, Friday or Saturday night the smell of coffee, now so necessary to life itself, may be held temporarily at bay at the West Bow, Candlemaker Row and the West Port by the heady aromatic cocktail of — you know — *cocktails*, made of improbable juices, and the spew thereof; lager, vodka (which triumphed over whisky at the bidding of the pod people), 'Lynx', tough gels and muds for man fringe, bad curry, worse pizza, pee, poo, phlegm, sweat, spit, sperm and mobile phones. Mobile phones have a stench.

Would you rather, you can hear people say, *would you rather* share the city with the noisome rabble of the XVIII century? Half out of their minds on whisky and small-beer and candle-wax and snuff and syphilis and pies stuffed with *God* knows what? Yes. I would. At least they made up their own minds.

SCIENCE FICTION OR SCIENCE FACT?

Coffee, the dark, corrosive semen of the Marketers from Outer Space has conquered everything. It's beaten out water, tea, beer, whisky and wine (don't make me laugh). It's conquered the human need for food: whenever a restaurant closes, it's replaced by a coffee shop. Or a pub, which is *then* replaced by a coffee shop. Coffee is everywhere, twenty-four hours a day. We literally live and breathe it and it keeps us marching in step with our alien marketing masters.

It's weird, isn't it? We nurture these delicate little fruits at a specially correct altitude. They can only grow in a few places in the balance of the world. Then we RIP them from their branches and banish them thousands of miles from their home. We roast them, scorch fuck out of them, shove them in a bag and vacuum suck 'em. We crush them, grind them, pulverize them, boil them, steam pressure them, drink the paltry fluid that is the result of all this backbreaking agony, and then throw it all in the trash as fast as damn it.

A love of truth demands the admission that the coffee brought to the city by the Beings is flavourful. Before, there were only Bird's and Camp coffee. READY-AYE-READY. We have been brought into the space age, a dawn of aesthetics, only to be killed. But the only really good coffee in the world is to be had at 'El Pato', Calle de los Hermanos Moroy, Logroño. That's in *Spain*, so forget it.

THE PRESENT COFFEE — DUALITY.

The existing coffee-duality may be explained in this way: it's in the architecture of our precious cultural institutions, right there in the fabric of the Usher Hall, where the function of the building (art, the important and adorable art of music) has been deemed *too beautiful*. And therefore subversive: so the building and its threatening function have been enclosed, cocooned, or as we said before the Usher Hall has been given a tumour, into which you rush at the interval, and where your mind is scrambled and derailed from art. And, conveniently, further huge sums of money are removed from your pocket, vast sums beyond the increasingly exorbitant amounts one has to pay for art in our city. So the real function of coffee is to destroy art, to ruin thought at the precise moment art should be apprehended, and to exhaust the purses of the people.

Amnesia and schizophrenia are the ultimate objects of the existing coffee-duality. Indeed, you might even view these coffee excrescences on our important buildings not merely as tumours but remoras. The symbiotic economy of the Usher Hall and its coffee-remora is now permanently joined.

(By the way, initial reports that the Debacle-Trams, conceived and constructed by the Marketer-Beings, actually run on coffee have thankfully been disproven. But what were we to think when we observed the suspicious number of cafes lining the scenically paltry yet lushly funded route of the Debacle-Trams?)

FLUSH WITH SUCCESS.

Since there is nothing to be done about this until the End of Time, or until the day some simple bacterium attacks all the Marketers in our town, there can be only one outcome. Enclose all Edinburgh in a typically ugly council-funded, architect-designed glass carapace, goitre or excresence. In fact, architects be damned — only a Claes Oldenburg would be able to effect the apotheosis of Edinburgh that the Marketers want: the city enclosed in a vast lavatory pan, twice daily filled to the gunwales with scalding Americano. After a decade or so of this scarifying, this near-drowning every day, we will have forgotten what our jobs are, who we are, even what art is. And that is just where the Marketers from Outer Space want us.

In the mornings the hundred thousand gallons of Americano will be flushed away with the collected piss of the stag and hen parties. At night with vodka. Or perhaps, in time, with song.

OLD-WORLD VERSE & SCOTTISH RENASCENCE: FLOURISHING EVERGREEN

ELIZABETH ELLIOTT

Describing the origins of the *Evergreen: A Northern Seasonal*, Patrick Geddes looks back to December 1894, when 'two or three of the young writers and artists of our little germ of a college, which had just before absorbed Allan Ramsay's old "goosepie" into its new buildings, gathered some of their own work and requisitioned some of their friends' into a Christmas Book and called it the "New Evergreen"'. As Geddes explains, 'This was, of course, in memory of Allan's "Evergreen" of 1724, a collection of simple verse, perhaps without great merit of their own, but which served [...] to suggest better things to others — in his case to no less than Percy, Burns, and Scott'. A collection of poetry, art, and essays, *The New Evergreen: The Christmas Book of University Hall* inspired the 'public and larger venture' of a periodical in four volumes, *Spring* (1895), *Autumn* (1895), *Summer* (1896), and *Winter* (1896–97).

In its various forms, Geddes' *Evergreen* is the product of his redevelopment of the poet, playwright, and wigmaker Allan Ramsay's former home at the top of the Royal Mile, known as the Goosepie in recognition of its unusual, octagonal shape. Having purchased the house in 1890, Geddes set it at the heart of his project of urban renewal, seeking to create a physical environment capable of nurturing an intellectual community, a place where academics, writers, artists, and other professions might be brought into a productive association, a genuine synthesis of 'town and gown'. Geddes' *Evergreen* articulates this social and cultural vision, yet the particular form this expression takes demands closer examination: lacking the popularity of the *Tea-Table Miscellany* (1724–37), Ramsay's *Ever Green* was not his most notable achievement. While the *Tea-Table Miscellany* became an ongoing venture, with three further volumes of traditional Scottish songs printed in multiple editions, the *Ever Green* failed to capture the imagination of a contemporary reading public, and only two of the four projected volumes ever saw the light of day. Why then did the inhabitants of Geddes' University Hall settle on the *Ever Green* as inspiration for their own publishing venture? This essay seeks to tease out some of the resonances of this choice, exploring the relationship between Ramsay's collection and Geddes' reciprocal work of material and cultural renewal.

Ramsay's own title stakes a claim to enduring fame for the poems collected within his *Ever Green*, drawn from the remarkable Bannatyne Manuscript, the single largest collection of poetry in English and Scots compiled in early modern Scotland, and finished in 1568. Taken from Pope's *Essay on Criticism*, the epigraph to volume one of Ramsay's *Ever Green* associates its contents with the perennial quality of the classical poets:

> Still green with Bays each ancient Altar stands
> Above the Reach of sacrilegious Hands,
> Secure from Flames, from Envys fiercer Rage
> Descructive War and all devouring Age.

Pope's lines gesture towards the part Ramsay's *Ever Green* itself is to play in preserving its poetic contents, and this sense of the collection's function is underlined in Ramsay's most notorious creative intervention in his medieval materials, the 'Postscript' that supplements William Dunbar's medieval poem 'I that in Heil wes'. Dunbar's poetic meditation on the inevitability of death and the hope for resurrection to eternal life is given a new twist in Ramsay's hands, as well as a more familiar title, 'A Lament for the Loss of the Poets'. Ramsay borrows Dunbar's voice to prophesy the role of his own major source, the Bannatyne Manuscript, and of the *Ever Green* itself in propagating a Scottish literary tradition. Complete with a footnote acknowledging Ramsay's patron, William Carmichael, for the loan of the Bannatyne Manuscript, the postscript anticipates Ramsay as 'a Lad' who will 'Revive our Fame and Memorie / Then sall we flourish EVIR GRENE'. In the role imagined here, Ramsay's collection serves the interests of literary conservation, renewing a tradition to be transmitted within a national empire: 'Far sall we fare, baith Eist and West / Owre ilka Clyme by Scots possest'.

Geddes' conception of Ramsay's *Ever Green*, as a collection of 'simple verse' that inspired Percy and Scott, marks a recognition of the collection's antiquarian function, and a sense of its place in the history of an engagement with the past that gave birth to medieval studies. Geddes' allusion to Scott in particular suggests an awareness not only of how Ramsay's activities shaped

Scott's conception of a popular literary tradition within Scotland, but perhaps also of Ramsay's role in bringing the Bannatyne Manuscript to public attention. As titular patron of the antiquarian printing society Scott founded in 1823, the Bannatyne Club, the manuscript's maker, George Bannatyne, plays a fundamental part in the foundation of Scottish studies. The Bannatyne Club's mission statement would later become the basis for the constitution of the Scottish Text Society (1882–): both originally defined their purpose as the publication of 'Works illustrative of the Scottish Language, Literature and History prior to the Union'.

For Geddes and his associates, however, the name of *Evergreen* held an appeal beyond its recollection of Scotland's literary past. The diverse contents of Geddes' *Evergreen*, where contributions from scientists and social scientists take their place alongside art and creative writing, represent a synthesis that disrupts the increasing tendency towards the fragmentation of knowledge into specialist disciplinary channels in the universities of Geddes' time. As Geddes argues, rather than being 'swept up into a Dryasdust Journal of their own', these academic distinctions 'all melt down for the *Evergreen* and weld into a chain, of which our individual essays are the links, and which I may call "The House the Sun Built"'. As Geddes' analogy suggests, the *Evergreen* appeals in its evocation of the natural growth stimulated by the sun, and the twin strands of growth and collaboration are connected through the conception of evolution Geddes explored with J. Arthur Thomson in *The Evolution of Sex*. For Geddes, evolution is 'not primarily through Struggle at the margin of subsistence', but 'primarily through Sex with its consequences of family and wider co-operation'. The productive intermixture of disciplines within the *Evergreen* mirrors the social exchange promoted between students, lecturers, and others within the community at Ramsay Garden, and the sense of the *Evergreen's* link to the idea of evolution is underlined in Geddes' account of its publication: 'there was no editor, indeed, nor hardly is yet, but what I may perhaps best describe as a struggle for existence'.

As an outgrowth from Geddes' project of urban redevelopment in Ramsay Garden, The *Evergreen* models Geddes' conception of the city as 'the organ of human evolution'. In *Coming Polity*, he writes of the city as, 'the vehicle of acquired inheritance. It accumulates and embodies the culture heritage of a region, and combines it in some measure and kind with the culture heritage of larger units, national, racial, religious, human [...] Like a photographic plate, the city receives the experiences of each passing generation and hands the record on to the next. It is the instrument primarily of the regional memory, but serves also as the memory of larger groups.'

The city's mnemonic function is 'far from passive', however, but 'also (and essentially) active, creative, evocatory. By some subtle alchemy, the spirit of the city selects and blends memories of the past with experiences of the present and hopes for the future.' As a creative synthesis of the memories of Edinburgh's past and the product of co-operative human effort, Geddes' *Evergreen* embodies his conception of the city as organ of human evolution in microcosmic form.

Geddes' sense of the reciprocity of memory, creativity, and urban development is articulated in his contribution to the first volume of *The Evergreen*, Spring. In 'The Scots Renascence', Geddes observes, 'When we remember how every movement — moral or social, industrial or spiritual — sooner or later takes architectural embodiment, we shall better understand the meaning both of the Old New Town and of this New Old one. We remember too how often architectural movements have accompanied and preceded literary ones.'

For Geddes, of 'the many traditions of the historic houses [...] none has been more inspiring, as none more persistently characteristic of Edinburgh than that of Allan Ramsay, who amid much other sowing and planting, edited an "Evergreen" in 1724.'

Ramsay's 'little collection of old-world verse, with its return at once to local tradition and living nature' is 'as little in harmony with the then existing fashion of the day in literature as its new namesake would hope to be with that of our own'. In contrast with 'the all-pervading "Decadence"' of his time, Geddes' *Evergreen* is framed as a tentative germination: an 'organic beginning' in need of fit time to 'survive and grow'; a 'replanting of the old poet's unsunned hillside'; the shivering of an 'early bud' as Spring breathes in the North. Vernal metaphors underline Geddes' sense that engagement with the past is an essential element in new growth, a means at once of living in the present and meeting the demands of the future.

Geddes' conception of the city as organ of human evolution and embodiment of cultural heritage suggests the extent to which his 1890s projects in Edinburgh's Old Town are not simply contemporaneous, but mutually reinforcing. Geddes' purchase of the Outlook Tower, now the Camera Obscura, in 1892, can be set alongside the construction work at Ramsay Garden, and the publication of the *Evergreen*. Visitors to the civic museum Geddes housed in this public observatory first met with the panoramic views of the city from the tower and the projected images supplied by the camera obscura, then moved through a series of exhibitions on each floor, spiraling outwards from the city through the nation, its language, Europe, and the world. As this progression implies, Geddes' concern with Edinburgh was not purely local. Geddes regarded the Outlook Tower as a prototype structure that might be introduced in other cities, enabling similar forms of productive engagement with the past, and a movement from the local to the universal: it was an 'amphitheatre of social evolution', where 'man's struggle for life' might be studied.

As material structures that facilitate reflection on cultural heritage, embodied within the urban environment, the Outlook Tower, Ramsay Garden, and the *Evergreen* fulfill reciprocal roles in Geddes' model of evolution. The Outlook Tower enables reflection on the urban fabric as an accretion of cultural heritage legible to those who have 'learned to read the concrete tide-marks of history, to interpret the strata laid down by each period, which are to the books called History, as the natural strata to the books of Geology'. The *Evergreen* too blends past memories with present experience and future expectations: in building on Ramsay's *Ever Green*, Geddes' publication recalls the ways in which Ramsay's anthology is itself a creative reworking of a multifarious Edinburgh tradition. Ramsay's major source, the Bannatyne Manuscript, was compiled in Edinburgh by George Bannatyne, then in his early twenties. Bannatyne claims to have transcribed his collection of poetry in the last three months of 1568, in time of plague when 'we fra labor was compeld to rest'. The sheer size of Bannatyne's anthology, together with alterations to dates given within the collection, lay his account of its production open to question, however. Bannatyne's manuscript reflects his own social position and the network of cultural contacts at his disposal, including family connections such as the poet Alexander Scott, whose poems appear alongside songs and other texts Bannatyne found in printed anthologies, and elsewhere. Alongside contemporary and anonymous work, we find medieval poems by Chaucer, Henryson, and Dunbar. Bannatyne presents his materials in a complex, and highly unusual, five-part arrangement by genre: devotional, moral, comic, love poems, and finally fables. Bannatyne's collection shapes his cultural heritage into a form that serves the interests of a community of 'reverend readers' addressed in a series of editorial poems. At the same time, the collection stakes Bannatyne's own claim to cultural capital, positioning him in an authoritative relationship to the aesthetic and moral values of his society.

In making his *Ever Green*, Allan Ramsay reformulated the materials of Bannatyne's collection, drawing overwhelmingly on his selection of comic poems to create an image of Scottish literature that emphasises Ramsay's ideal of 'Strength of Thought and Simplicity of Stile'. Ramsay depicts the *Ever Green* poets as 'good old Bards', whose 'poetry is the Product of their own Country, not pilfered and spoiled in the Transportation from abroad: Their Images are native, and their Landskip domestick, copied from those Fields and Meadows we every day behold'. Although Ramsay's collection encompasses the poetry of a courtly elite, influenced by European tradition, the accent of his *Ever Green* falls on comic poems of rural life and labour, such as 'The Wife of Auchtermuchty'. Ramsay's version of Scottish literature is one that anticipates his own use of vernacular Scots as the basis of a poetry that represents the lives of working people. Creative additions and elaborations expose the extent to which Ramsay's *Ever Green* is a conscious reworking of the literary past: Ramsay's *Vision*, for example, is a pastiche of medieval dream vision poetry. Presented to the reader as a fourteenth-century Latin poem translated in the sixteenth century, the *Vision* adopts the mode of prophecy to offer a timely reflection on Scotland's past and future prospects as an independent nation.

Awakening the echoes of an Edinburgh tradition that connects to the national past, Patrick Geddes' nineteenth-century *Evergreen* draws in its wake the memory of Walter Scott's Bannatyne Club, whose printing of 'Works illustrative' of Scotland's past fosters a distinctive sense of Scottish identity in a wider British context. Geddes' own sense of Scotland's cultural specificity is fully compatible with membership of the British Union and internationalism: for him 'the older loves and kinships, the smaller nationality' do not demand rejection of 'our part in the larger responsibilities of united nationality and race'. The Celticism of his Celtic Revival celebrates the interconnecting identities of Wales, Ireland, and France, rather than Scotland alone, and the united diversity of pieces within *The Evergreen* speak to this sense of shared Celtic identity, in pieces from John Duncan's *Anima Celtica* to Edith Wingate Rinder's 'Amel and Penhor (A Breton Legend)'. Other pieces address the more localised past of the Bannatynian tradition represented by Ramsay's *Ever Green*: Charles Hodge Mackie's image *Robene and Makyn* offers a visual interpretation of Robert Henryson's comic pastoral poem about a shepherd's botched wooing. Elsewhere, Pittendrigh Macgillivray's 'Ane Playnt of Luve' recalls the creative appropriations of the past carried out by Ramsay and Scott's Bannatynians, in ventriloquising the language and experience of Older Scots as the medium of new work. The link between the *Evergreen* as a structure raised on the foundation of Ramsay's work and the Geddesian development of Ramsay Garden is reinforced by continuities within their decorative schemes: as Victor Brandford observes, decorations 'are the visible link that connect the *Evergreen* with the builder's craft [...] They are to a considerable extent simple transcriptions into black and white of detached parts from the series of mural decorations which the artists, temporarily turned craftsmen, have painted on various walls of University Hall'. In taking Allan Ramsay's *Ever Green* as inspiration for a series of publications celebrating an urban development and a communal mode of life, Geddes and his collaborators articulate the city's function as living organ of evolution, bearing witness not only to the history of Edinburgh's productive engagement with the past, but pointing towards the possible ways in which that past might shape humanity's future.

PRESS

The spring Evergreen, brought out
by Geddes and Colleagues in 1895
was wrapped in brown calf suede
as if born and bound to the season.

My copy is falling to bits, and yet
I would never part with its pages,
read and used over a century ago
as a wild flower press, sending

halos of colours bleeding through
poems and prose. Not one flower
that those dead hands gathered
and then preserved has died out,

neither are they considered weeds,
but many have spread in the field.

Richie McCaffery

C O N T R I B U T O R S

Leila Aboulela's latest novel, *Lyrics Alley,* was Fiction Winner of the Scottish Book Awards. She lives in Aberdeen.

Dominic Cooper has written four novels and now lives in the West Highlands where he works as a watchmaker.

Christine De Luca, Edinburgh's current Makar, writes in both English and Shetlandic. Her most recent collection is *Dat Trickster Sun* (Mariscat, 2014).

Kate Downie is a Scottish landscape artist whose career over the past 30 years has spanned the media of painting, drawing, printmaking, performance and film. Her work appears in public & private collections worldwide.

Elizabeth Elliott is a lecturer in English Literature at the University of Aberdeen. Her research focuses on the cultural influence of the Bannatyne Manuscript and its Evergreen legacy.

Robin Gillanders is former Reader in Photography at Edinburgh Napier University. He has published and exhibited frequently and internationally.

Alan Gillis's fourth collection *Scapegoat* is published by The Gallery Press in October 2014.

David Herd's collections of poetry include *All Just* (Carcanet) and *Outwith* (Bookthug). His work has appeared in various international journals, including Blackbox Manifold, Like Starlings, Mascara, nY and Otoliths.

Stuart Kelly is a writer and critic. He was a Man Booker judge in 2013 and is the author of *The Book Of Lost Books.*

Peter Kravitz was born in London in 1961 and has lived mostly in Scotland. His grandparents came from Poland. His parents and sisters were born in Union City, New Jersey.

Richie McCaffery is the author of two poetry pamphlets and one collection, Cairn. He is finishing a PhD in Scottish Literature at the University of Glasgow.

Ian McDonough's latest collection - A Witch Among the Gooseberries is published by Mariscat in November. He lives in Edinburgh where he manages the Scottish Community Mediation Centre.

Andrew MacDougall was born in Edinburgh and works in Human Resources in the cultural heritage sector.

Todd McEwen was born in California. For that reason alone he supports Scottish Independence. His next book is The Projection Room.

John McGlade is a performance poet from Glasgow who also scripts comedy material for television, radio and theatre.

Marcas Mac An Tuairneir's collection of poetry, Deò (Breath) was published in 2013 by Grace Note Publications. His second, Lus na Tùise (Lavender), will arrive this year. Chaidh Deò, a' chiad chruinneachadh bàrdachd aig Marcas Mac an Tuairneir, fhoillseachadh ann an 2013 aig Grace Note Publications. Nochdaidh an dàrna chruinneachadh aige, Lus na Tùise, am bliadhna.

Benjamin Morris is a writer and researcher from Mississipi whose work appears regularly in the US and Europe. He lives in New Orleans.

Robert Morris spent all his tax paying life in Scotland and remains professor emeritus, having taught economic and social history for many years at Edinburgh University.

Owen O'Neill is a playwright, comedian and poet. His new collection of poetry and short stories Licking the Matchbox was published in 2014.

John Reiach is an Edinburgh-based photographer influenced here by Eric de Maré's 1950's black-and-white post cards exploring the relationship between buildings and landscape.

Mario Relich is Secretary of the Poetry Association of Scotland. His first book of poems *Frisky Ducks* (Grace Note Publications) is published this year.

James Robertson's books include *The Testament of Gideon Mack*, *And the Land Lay Still*, *The Professor of Truth* and *365*.

Professor Richard Rodger has written extensively on the history of Edinburgh (*The Transformation of Edinburgh*; *Edinburgh's Colonies* and *Insanitary City*).

Mike Saunders has been published in various journals including Lighthouse, Poetry Review, Gutter and the Istanbul Review. He lives in Edinburgh.

Morelle Smith is a poet, fiction and travel writer with a particular interest in the Balkans.

Nancy Somerville's first poetry collection, *Waiting for Zebras* was published by Red Squirrel Press (Scotland) in 2008.

Jock Stein is a preacher, piper and poet living in Haddington, East Lothian.

David Tomassini is a Scottish writer and translator who has been living and working in Italy for 30 years.

Samantha Walton's poetry pamphlets are *Amaranth*, *Unstitched*, *City Break Weekend Songs* and *tristanundisolde* (as Posie Rider).